Gourmet Tortillas

Exotic and Traditional Tortilla Dishes

Karen Howarth

Clear Light Publishers
Santa Fe, New Mexico

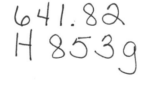

Clear Light Publishers
823 Don Diego
Santa Fe, New Mexico 87501
www.clearlightbooks.com

First Edition
10 9 8 7 6 5 4 3 2 1

Library of Congress Cataloging-in-Publication Data

Howarth, Karen, 1958-
Gourmet tortillas : exotic and traditional dishes / by Karen Howarth
p. cm.
ISBN 1-57416-058-3
1. Tortillas. I. Title
TX770.T65 H69 2000
641.8′2–dc21

00-064538

Edited by Joan Stromquist
Book design by Carl Stromquist
Cover art & drawings by John B. Crane, Sandhill Studios, Santa Fe, NM
Previously published by Tierra Publications.
Printed in Canada

Each tortilla pictured on the cover represents a recipe in this book. From top to bottom: *Jalapeño Tortillas, Orange Tortillas with Montmorency Cherries,* and *Lavender Tortillas with Garlic Chives.*

Table of Contents

About the Author

My love for cooking began in a small farming town in Michigan, where the Amish still tie their buggies to the parking meters on Main Street. The two restaurants in Gladwin provided plenty of homestyle cooking, but cuisines which strayed from the typical Midwestern meal of meat and potatoes were absent. Luckily for me, a daughter of avid travelers, I was exposed to international cuisines by dining in some of the finest restaurants in the United States, Portugal, Mexico and the Caribbean. At the time, I didn't realize that vivid memories of bittersweet Swiss chocolate, crusty European hard rolls and homemade Mexican tortillas would influence my cooking style for a lifetime.

Around the age of ten I began my culinary career with a clever attempt to avoid my most dreaded chore ..... washing the dinner dishes! My mother agreed to let me prepare the evening meal in exchange for cleaning up the kitchen afterwards. This arrangement made it possible for me to play with my friends after eating, with the added benefit of choosing my favorite meals. I loved it because it was fun, and the praise I received was gratifying. Each year since then, my love and motivation to cook creatively has grown, and so has the pile of dishes which I thought I had so cleverly escaped.

After moving to the Pacific Northwest about fifteen years ago, I became interested in, and eventually hooked on, making flour tortillas. It all started one day when I was hit with a sudden craving for a Cheddar cheese tortilla. I searched every cookbook available for tortilla recipes and could only find two ..... one for white flour and one for whole wheat. The ingredients consisted of flour, salt, baking powder, lard and water. Guided by my experience with embellished yeast breads, I decided to alter the white flour recipe. First I replaced the lard with butter, a taste I prefer, and then added finely grated, sharp Cheddar cheese. This produced a tortilla with a delicious cheese flavor, a speckled appearance and a slightly chewy texture. My family devoured them! So I made the tortillas again and served them at a big, neighborhood potluck party. They were the hit of the evening! From that point on I was inspired to create tortillas embellished with an array of new flavors and textures. Ripening scallions turned into *Scallion Tortillas,* forgotten cottage cheese became *Cottage*

cheese became *Cottage Cheese Tortillas,* and leftover mashed potatoes were transformed into *Sour Cream & Potato Tortillas*. I then began to incorporate these wonderful new tortilla discoveries into many exotic and traditional dishes, the best of which are included in this cookbook.

Tortillas are fun to make and easy to roll. They are much more forgiving to work with than pastry or pie crusts. My youngest daughter has been rolling tortillas since she was three years old. At age five, it is difficult to distinguish her tortillas from mine. Making a batch of eight tortillas will take only about 45 minutes from start to finish, including the 15 minutes needed to rest the dough. Begin your experience with *Yogurt Tortillas (recipe page 66)* or *Traditional Flour Tortillas (recipe page 64),* as both yield dough which is especially easy to work with. And the tortillas don't have to be perfectly round ..... that's part of their charm!

Karen Howarth

About the Artist

"Spend more time looking at your subject than at your drawing, and remember ..... keep your pencil *sharp*, so that if you touch your finger with it, you draw blood!" These pointed words from my high school art teacher were pivotal to my transition from a preschooler who doodled on everything in sight to a professional artist, getting paid for what I love doing most. Always inspired by the beauty of the outdoors, I learned to combine art and nature with a realism that comes only from intense observation of color, line, light, shadow and shape. The lay of petals on the stem of a flower, the wrinkling of skin around a whale's eye, or the folds of a tortilla in a burrito ..... all are objects of fascination which I try to render with the greatest care and accuracy.

Together with my wife Ann, our dogs Maxine and Nikki, and Sam the cat, I live and work in beautiful Santa Fe, New Mexico. How lucky I feel to have my childhood dream become a reality.

John B. Crane

About Tortillas

Gourmet tortillas have been enjoyed for over 9000 years! The ancient Indian tribes of Southern Mexico often added tender leaves of wild buckwheat, ash and mustard greens to their tortilla dough. Madroños flowers, when in season, were added for spice. Canyon figs and toasted Iresine seeds were pulverized and ground, then mixed into the tortilla dough before it was baked. These wild grasses and native plants improved the flavor, texture and nutritional value of their tortillas.

Today, in Southern Mexico corn tortillas are eaten exclusively. The Northern States of Mexico enjoy flour tortillas in addition to traditional corn tortillas. From personal observation, I notice Americans enjoy light, leavened tortillas made with white or whole wheat flour. My favorite grocery store allocates only two feet of refrigerator space for corn tortillas, in contrast to the twenty feet of space for flour tortillas! Even the largest selection of various brands, however, cannot compare with homemade. The "best" tortillas are made fresh, at home, and enriched with an array of flavors like jalapeño chile peppers, sharp Cheddar cheese or sun-dried tomatoes.

My love for gourmet tortillas gives me a sense of kinship with the ancient Aztec Indians. Although the ingredients I use are considerably different, the concept is still the same. Tortillas have stood the test of time, favored for thousands of years, creating a solid foundation to build upon. The human palate craves variety and complexity, and with the current ease of access to exotic and foreign foods, the opportunity for exciting results from our imagination is phenomenal.

Karen Howarth

About Making Tortillas

At first glance, the directions for making homemade tortillas may appear lengthy. Yet after making them once or twice, you will easily commit the procedure to memory.

There is very little kitchen equipment needed to make tortillas, but I do suggest reading the directions thoroughly before you begin, just in case. With a little experience, you'll soon be able to refer only to the simplified directions in colored type at the beginning of each step.

Have fun in the process, let the kids help if they want to, and remember, homemade tortillas don't have to be perfectly round ..... that's part of their charm!

1. Sift the ingredients into a medium bowl.

Place a flour sifter in a medium-size bowl. *(A wide, shallow bowl will allow you to knead the dough right in the bowl.)* Place the flour, baking powder and salt into the sifter, and sift.

2. Cut the butter into the flour until the mixture resembles coarse meal.

Use a pastry cutter or your fingers. Vegetable shortening may be substituted for butter in all recipes.

3. Add the liquid(s) to the flour mixture all at once and mix well.

When measuring liquids, use a one-cup, glass measuring cup that is calibrated in ounces as well as fractions. This book uses both calibrations, since it allows for more accurate measurements.

4. Gather the dough into a ball with your hands and knead briefly.

Different brands of flour will absorb different amounts of liquid, so your dough might need slightly less iiquid than the recipe calls for.

(continued on next page)

If there is still flour left in the bowl, after the majority of the dough has been gathered into a soft ball: Set the ball of dough aside and add very small amounts of water *(a teaspoon at a time)* to the remaining flour mixture until it also can be gathered into a soft ball. Combine the 2 balls of dough by kneading briefly.

If the dough is slightly sticky: Knead in small amounts of flour *(a teaspoon at a time)* until the dough is soft but no longer sticky.

5. Divide the dough into equal pieces.

8	pieces for 8" tortillas
10	pieces for 7" tortillas
16	pieces for 5" tortillas
36	pieces for 3" tortillas
72	pieces for 1" tortillas *(or prepare half the tortilla recipe and then divide the dough into 36 pieces)*

6. Form each piece into a smooth ball and flatten slightly with your hands.

7. Cover with a towel and let rest for 15 minutes.

Place the pieces of dough on one side of a clean dish towel and cover them with the other side of the towel. Let the dough rest 15 minutes.

8. Preheat a dry, heavy skillet over medium heat.

My stove is calibrated on a 1 *(low)* to 9 *(high)* scale. I cook tortillas on 3½. Be sure to let the pan preheat for at least 5 minutes before cooking the first tortilla; a cast iron pan will take a little longer.

9. On a lightly floured board, roll out 1 piece into a circle.

Place a wooden cutting board close to the stove. Sprinkle lightly with flour *(about ½ teaspoon per tortilla)*. Place 1 piece of dough on the floured board. Turn the dough over so that both sides are lightly covered with flour.

With a wooden rolling pin, gently roll the dough from the center outward, moving around the circle until you arrive at the desired diameter *(refer to step number 5)*. Tortillas don't have to be perfectly round. Only mechanically produced tortillas have such a uniform appearance.

10. Cook the tortilla on a dry skillet until lightly browned on both sides.

Cook the tortilla for 45 to 60 seconds on one side. The tortilla is ready to be turned over when it is lightly browned on the bottom and slightly bubbly on top. Use your fingers *(or a spatula)* to turn it over.

While the first side of the tortilla is cooking, begin to roll out the next tortilla. When the next tortilla is half rolled out, it will be time to turn the first tortilla over. Be sure that the bottom is lightly browned before turning. When you finish rolling out the second tortilla, the first tortilla should be done. Remove the first tortilla, now lightly browned on both sides, from the heat.

11. Stack the cooked tortillas on a wire rack to cool slightly.

The other cooked tortillas will be stacked on top of the first one. Continue rolling and cooking until all of the tortillas are cooked.

12. Package the tortillas while still warm.

Let the tortillas cool slightly, about 5 minutes, after making the last tortilla. Then package them in a sealable plastic bag while still warm. Store the tortillas at room temperature, in the refrigerator, or in the freezer.

About Keeping Tortillas

Packaging and Storing Tortillas

Package the tortillas while still warm, in a sealed plastic bag or plastic container. Prevent the top tortilla from becoming damp *(from condensation)* by placing a paper towel on the top tortilla. Remove the damp paper towel when the tortillas are completely cooled. Store tortillas at room temperature for up to 3 days.

Tortillas also can be stored in the refrigerator for up to 7 days, or in the freezer for up to 3 months.

Reheating Tortillas

Wrap the tortillas in a large piece of foil, and place in a 300° oven for 5 to 15 minutes, depending on how many tortillas are being warmed. Tortillas also may be reheated in a microwave oven, but be careful not to overheat them or they will become stiff and chewy. Steaming cooked, homemade tortillas is not recommended. They become damp and soggy. It is unnecessary to reheat fresh tortillas when making enchiladas, or other dishes with rolled tortillas. Fresh tortillas will retain their flexibility even when cool.

About "Imperfect" Tortillas

Dough is hard to roll

The amount of liquid necessary to make a soft dough varies with the brand of flour you use. Some brands of flour absorb more liquids than others. When the flour can absorb more liquid than a recipe calls for, leave the excess flour in the bowl. If you attempt to combine the excess flour into the dough, the result will be a stiff, elastic, hard to roll dough. Next time, add 1 to 2 tablespoons of water to the amount of liquid called for in the recipe, and add the liquids all at once.

Let the dough rest at least 15 minutes before rolling out the tortillas. This allows the gluten in the flour to become less elastic and makes the dough easier to roll out.

Dough has an uneven thickness while rolling

Lift the tortilla up while rolling to check for thick spots. Place the tortilla back on the wooden board and roll gently, from the center outward, over the thick areas until the tortilla is a uniform thickness. Raising the tortilla up off the board also allows the dough to slide more freely and to be rolled more quickly.

Dough has an uneven shape while rolling

Raise the dough up off the board several times while rolling. The elastic nature of the dough causes the tortilla to become more circular when it has been removed from the rolling surface. Reposition the tortilla on the rolling surface and gently roll, from the center outward, in the direction where the tortilla needs to become more circular. Raising the tortilla off the board will allow the dough to slide more freely and to be rolled more quickly.

(continued on next page)

Tortilla sticks while cooking

Some embellished tortillas *(containing Cheddar cheese, cottage cheese, olives, etc.)* may stick slightly and require a spatula to turn them over.

Dough is too wet

Recombine the remaining balls of dough to form 1 large ball. Knead in small amounts of flour *(1 teaspoon at a time),* until the dough is no longer sticky.

Always use a dry, well seasoned, cast iron skillet or a non-stick pan for cooking tortillas. Do not oil or spray the pan with non-stick sprays if the tortillas stick. Instead, refer to the above suggestions.

Cooked tortillas are doughy

The tortilla is undercooked. Reduce the temperature and allow several minutes for the pan to cool down to the new temperature. Cook the remaining tortillas for a few seconds longer *(on each side)* than was done initially.

Cooked tortillas taste floury

Use a little less flour when rolling out the tortillas. If the dough is too sticky to roll out with less flour, recombine the dough to make 1 large ball and knead in a little flour *(1 teaspoon at a time)* until the dough is no longer sticky. Redivide the dough and let it rest for another 15 minutes. Roll out the remaining tortillas using a smaller amount of flour *(only about ¼ to ½ teaspoon for each tortilla)* than was done initially.

Wipe off the tortillas that are already cooked with a clean, damp cloth to remove the excess flour.

Tortillas are too thick after cooking

Dry doughs become very elastic while cooking. They will contract more than usual, creating a smaller, thicker tortilla. Dry doughs are also hard to roll out; for better results see suggestions listed under *Dough is hard to roll.*

Cooked tortillas are stiff

Tortillas that are cooked too slowly become stiff and will crack easily when rolled or folded. Cook the remaining tortillas at a slightly higher temperature and for several seconds less on each side. Allow several minutes for the pan to heat to the new temperature.

Package the tortillas in a sealed plastic bag or plastic container while still warm to retain softness. To prevent condensation from making the top tortilla wet, place a paper towel on the top and remove it when the tortillas are cool.

When reheating tortillas in a microwave oven, heat only until warm. Excess heating will cause the tortilla to become stiff and chewy.

Tortillas crack after storage

Tortillas retain their freshness for about 3 days. Tortillas older than this, as well as refrigerated tortillas, should be reheated before use to avoid cracking.

Tortillas need to be laid flat during storage. Wherever the edges are curled up, the tortilla will crack and break off. Also refer to above suggestions listed under *Cooked tortillas are stiff*.

About Children & Tortillas

Tortillas are as popular with children as they are with adults. In fact, I've had more success serving tortillas to finicky young guests than I've had with any other food ..... even pizza!

Creating tortillas is an enjoyable experience for children, even toddlers. There seems to be a natural fascination with tortilla dough because kids can push it, poke it, play with it, and eventually eat it. My children, Emily and Sara, both began to play with tortilla dough at a very young age. It was a self-serving gesture on my part, allowing me to be creative in the kitchen, while at the same time keeping them entertained. I quickly realized the educational benefits resulting from Emily and Sara's participation. We have conversations about fractions, heat, chemical reactions, following directions, cooperation and the list goes on.

After cooking with children of all ages and temperaments, I've made a few observations and learned a few tricks that make the process flow smoothly. Perhaps they will be of some assistance to you and your children. The lessons learned and skills acquired, at an early age, will last a lifetime and are well worth a little bit of spilled flour!

Toddlers

Choose a time when your toddlers are not hungry, so they will be less likely to eat the dough. Place a highchair close to your workspace to allow them to see what you are doing. Give your toddler a very small piece of dough to play with while you roll out the tortillas.

3 to 5 year olds

Place your child's step stool close to your workspace, a safe distance from the stove. *(I place myself between the stove and the child.)* Pre-measure all of the ingredients and place them out of arm's reach ..... otherwise they may be added sooner than you'd think! Preschool children enjoy stirring, pouring and mixing. They also enjoy playing with small pieces of dough and sampling the first cooked tortilla.

6 to 10 year olds

School age children like to measure the ingredients. Use dry measuring cups, showing your child how to level the dry ingredients by running one finger across the top of the cup. When measuring liquids or using measuring spoons, have the child measure over a separate container, in case they pour too much. School age children can begin to practice rolling their own tortillas. The resulting tortillas will be of various shapes, and probably small - about 4 inches in diameter.

11 years old and older

Let older children select the recipe they want to make. As your child's rolling skills improve, the tortillas will become more rounded and larger, up to 7 or 8 inches in diameter. Under close supervision, older children can cook their own tortillas. Be sure to provide them with a spatula for turning the tortillas over.

Best tortillas to make with children

Buttermilk Tortillas (recipe page 36), Campground Tortillas (recipe page 38), Risen (Yeast) Tortillas (recipe page 54), Steamed Tortillas (recipe page 62), Traditional Flour Tortillas (recipe page 64), or *Yogurt Tortillas (recipe page 66)*

Best tortilla dishes to make with children

Cheese Quesadillas (recipe page 76), Fried Olives (recipe page 74), Cheese Burritos with Spicy Frijoles (recipe page 100), Corn Chowder with Tortilla Crackers (recipe page 84), Pizza Quesadillas (recipe page 78), Soft Tostada (recipe page 133), Steamed Botana (recipe page 80), or *Tortilla Snowflakes (recipe page 82)*

(continued on next page)

Tortillas enjoyed by children

Applesauce Tortillas (recipe page 30), Black Olive & Sour Cream Tortillas (recipe page 33), Cheddar Cheese Tortillas (recipe page 39), Cream Cheese Tortillas (recipe page 43), Oatmeal Tortillas (recipe page 47), or *Orange Tortillas with Montmorency Cherries (recipe page 48)*

Tortilla dishes enjoyed by children

Asiago Fettucine (recipe page 135), Breakfast Burrito (recipe page 104), Cheese Enchiladas (recipe page 108), Chicken Enchiladas (recipe page 109), Nacho Appetizers (recipe page 77), Kiwi Chicken Burritos (recipe page 102), Macaroni & Three Cheese Pie (recipe page 134), Sunny-Side Up Fried Rice Over Tortillas (recipe page 130), or *Tortilla Buffet (recipe page 147)*

For breakfast

Serve warm, lightly buttered tortillas sprinkled with cinnamon sugar, powdered sugar or maple sugar, drizzled with honey, to be dipped in warm maple syrup, with jam or marmalade, or filled with scrambled eggs.

For lunch

Serve peanut butter and jelly roll-ups, open-face peanut butter tortillas decorated with sliced kiwi and bananas, bologna and cheese, hot dogs, sloppy joes, hamburgers *(form the ground beef into rectangles before cooking),* or a grilled cheese "sandwich" cut into wedges before serving.

About Tortilla Sandwiches

Gourmet tortillas will add a new sensation of colors, flavors and textures to your favorite sandwiches. Virtually any sandwich can be made and improved by substituting tortillas for bread. Family and guests enjoy the escape from the mundane! As a source of inspiration, I've compiled a few suggestions for you, along with some helpful hints. Fire up your imagination and create your own tortilla sandwich!

Best Tortillas for Sandwiches

Choose from *Beer Tortillas (recipe page 32), Butter Tortillas (recipe page 35), Cheddar Cheese Tortillas (recipe page 39), Jalapeño Tortillas (recipe page 44), Oatmeal Tortillas (recipe page 47), Parmesan Tortillas (recipe page 49), Potato Tortillas (recipe page 50), Risen (Yeast) Tortillas (recipe page 54), Scallion Tortillas (recipe page 57), Sourdough Tortillas (recipe page 60), Sun-Dried Tomato Tortillas (recipe page 61), Traditional Flour Tortillas (recipe page 64), Whole Wheat Tortillas (recipe page 65), or Yogurt Soda Tortillas (recipe page 67)*

Tortillas for sandwiches are best when fresh.

Club Sandwich

Spread a small amount of mayonnaise over the entire tortilla. Top with slices of turkey, Cheddar cheese and tomato. Spread a small amount of mayonnaise over the second tortilla *(a different flavor if you like* and place the tortilla over the tomato slices. Top with crisp bacon, sliced Swiss cheese and lettuce. Top with another tortilla and cut into wedges before serving.

Reuben Sandwich

Place thinly sliced corned beef over the entire tortilla. Top with a thin layer of well drained sauerkraut and sliced Swiss cheese. Broil 1 to 2 minutes, or until the cheese begins to brown. Remove from heat. Fold tortilla in half before serving. Serve with a small bowl of Dijon mustard.

(continued on next page)

Warm Meats

Choose from grilled chicken, meat loaf, roast beef with gravy, turkey, bacon, bratwurst, sliced prime rib served with au jus, teriyaki beef, or grilled ham.

Cold Meats

Choose from chicken, turkey, sliced ham, ham salad, roast beef, salami, bologna, or corned beef.

Spread a thin layer of mustard, horseradish, mayonnaise, etc. over ⅓ of the tortilla. Place the sliced meat on the same ⅓ of the tortilla. Top with cheese, tomatoes, olives, or lettuce. Roll the tortilla up beginning with the side that contains the meat.

Fish and Seafood

Choose from Alaskan halibut, cod, salmon, lake trout, tuna fish salad *(if possible, made with fresh tuna),* crab salad, or shrimp salad.

Fish filets can be grilled, baked in parchment paper, broiled or deep-fried. They can also be marinated or breaded before cooking. Place fish filet on one side of a tortilla, drizzle fish with fresh lemon juice and a dash of salt and seasoned pepper. Fold tortilla over fish filet before serving.

Sliced Cheeses

Use Provolone, Cheddar, Swiss, Jarlsberg, American, Monterey Jack, or Havarti.

Sliced cheese works well when making cold sandwiches; grated cheeses tend to spill out. Cut the cheese into 1" to 2" strips for easier rolling.

Grated Cheeses

Use Mozzarella, Provolone, Asiago, freshly grated Parmesan or Romano, Cheddar, Monterey Jack, Fontina, or Swiss.

Grated cheese works well when you are planning to melt the cheese. Use any of the cheeses listed above. Cheddar cheese will have a less oily texture when mixed with one of the other cheeses such as Monterey Jack, Provolone, or Mozzarella.

Wrap cheese filled tortillas in foil and heat in a 300° oven for 10 to 15 minutes.

Or, heat in a microwave oven *(unwrapped)* just until the cheese begins to melt, about 30 seconds. Be careful not to heat them too long or the tortilla will become chewy and stiff.

Spreadable Cheeses

Try cream cheese *(plain or with minced fresh chives)* or Brie.

Fill warmed tortillas just prior to serving.

Lettuce

Use whole leaves of romaine lettuce, curly endive and other varieties of leaf lettuce.

If shredded lettuce is needed, use iceberg. Just before serving, cut the head of lettuce into quarters, remove several of the yellow leaves in the center and slice thinly.

Tomatoes

Use finely sliced or diced plum tomatoes; they have less seeds and pulp than other tomatoes. Or, remove pulp with your fingers and discard, then coarsely dice the flesh.

Chile Peppers

Try anaheim, chipotle, jalapeño, or canned green chiles *(well drained)*.

Choose from fresh or roasted chile peppers. Grocery stores are now carrying fresh chiles that have been roasted and peeled. Try them for a distinctly different flavor. Top sandwiches with finely minced or thinly sliced chile peppers or garnish with a whole, small chile pepper.

See page 23 for a comprehensive description of most chile peppers and their characteristics.

(continued on next page)

The Onion Family

Try minced scallions, fresh chives, very thinly sliced sweet onions *(preferably Walla Walla or Vidalia),* sliced and sautéed yellow or white onions.

Pickled Delicacies

Choose from a wide variety of dill pickles, jalapeño pickles, sweet pickles, watermelon pickles, mustard pickles, black or green olives, capers, corn relish, or pickle relish.

Other Vegetables

Try mashed or sliced avocado, cucumbers *(I like the less seedy English cucumbers sliced thinly with cream cheese and a dash of black pepper),* bean or alfalfa sprouts, or thinly sliced red or green bell pepper *(fresh or sautéed in butter)*.

Sauces and Condiments

Choose from tomato salsa, cactus salsa, cherry salsa, sour cream, Dijon mustard, catsup, mayonnaise, gravy, or beef au jus.

When making sandwiches with gravy or sauces, place meat on ⅓ of the tortilla, fold up the bottom ⅓, then roll up the tortilla. This will help prevent leakage when eating the sandwich. Sauces can also be used for dipping; a rolled-up tortilla is the perfect shape for it!

About Chile Peppers

Americans have discovered the excitement of hot and spicy foods, and as a result, the use of chile peppers *(genus Capsicum)* has exploded in popularity. There are up to 200 identified varieties, each one with a unique taste and quality of heat. Chiles can be purchased fresh, dried, frozen, canned, crushed and powdered. When working with any form of chile peppers, remember to be careful not to touch your eyes with your hands because the heat will burn them. Many people use rubber gloves when handling chiles. If you eat a bite of food that is too hot, the best antidote for the heat is a dairy product such as milk, yogurt, ice cream, or a starch, such as rice or tortillas. Contrary to popular opinion, cold beer and water do not work!

How to Roast Chile Peppers

Place the peppers on a rack over a gas flame, on a grill, or under a broiler. The skin should blacken and blister all over. Do this quickly, so the flesh won't burn. Then place the peppers in a bowl, cover it with plastic wrap, and let the peppers "sweat" for about 10 minutes so that the skin loosens. Pull the skin off with your fingers. If the skin sticks, gently scrape it off with the back of a knife blade. Don't wash the peppers. Remove the seeds with a spoon or the tip of a knife.

Types of Chile Peppers

Anaheim: Long, green chile, similar to the New Mexico green chile, only milder and not as sharply defined in flavor. Excellent roasted. Good stuffed, in stews and sauces. Widely available. Mild heat.

Ancho: A dried red-ripe poblano chile, 3 to 5 inches long and 2 to 4 inches wide. Reddish brown in color and very wrinkled. The most commonly used dried chile in Mexico. Sweet, with a fruity flavor of cherries and dried plums. Medium hot.

(continued on next page)

Arbol: Small dried red chiles, usually serrano, but sometimes cayenne or Thai chiles. Good toasted. Widely available. Extremely hot.

Bell, green: Bright green, sweet and mild. Good stuffed and baked, grilled, or roasted. Available everywhere. No heat.

Bell, red: Very sweet and crisp. Good raw, grilled and roasted. Almost always available. No heat.

Bell, yellow: Sweet, crisp and fruity. Usually available. No heat.

Cascabel: Dried version of a Mexican chile, which, when ripe, looks like an Italian cherry pepper. Nutty-sweet flavor. Good toasted whole in oil. Medium hot.

Cayenne: Bright red dried pepper, 2 to 4 inches long and ½ inch across. Pungent heat. Can be used whole in soups, stews and sauces, but usually are sold ground as a seasoning powder. Very hot.

Chile Caribe: Crushed dried New Mexican red chile peppers. Comes packed in bags labeled as "crushed red chile flakes". Medium to hot.

Chile Molido: Ground dried New Mexican red chile peppers. Varies in flavor and heat.

Chimayó Red Chile Powder: Ground dried red chiles from Chimayó, New Mexico. Highly prized for its excellent flavor. Hot, smoky, sweet and nutty. Mild to hot.

Chipotle, dried: A smoked jalapeño, 2 to 4 inches long, light dusty brown in color. Good toasted. Used in soups and salsas. Very hot.

Chipotle, in adobo sauce: Canned, dried, smoked jalapeños that are simmered in a tomato-vinegar sauce. Widely available. Very hot.

Green (New Mexico): Fresh, related to the anaheim, but with a much fuller flavor. Wonderful roasted. Used in sauces, stews, soups, or just eaten plain. Comes frozen or canned in most markets, but fresh is far superior. Frozen is preferred to canned. Also known as "Hatch". Mild to hot.

Guajillo: Dried red chile, about 4 inches long and reddish brown in color. Nutty-rich flavor. Good in salsas and moles. Mildly hot.

Habanero: Fresh, dark green, or orange to red. About 2 inches long and 1½ inches wide. One of the hottest chiles in the world. Distinct flavor. Goes well with tropical fruits and tomatoes. Fierce heat!

Jalapeño: Fresh, dark green chile, about 2 to 3 inches long. The most popular chile in the United States. Readily available. Excellent raw or roasted. Also available in red and yellow. Medium to high heat.

Japone: Small, thin dried red chiles with a unique, sharp heat. Thai or arbol chiles may be substituted. Very hot.

Morita: A type of dried smoked jalapeño with a sweet, smoky flavor. Used in soups and salsas. Medium-high heat.

Mulato: A type of dried poblano. Dark brown with a slight licorice and tobacco flavor. Used in moles, sauces, stews and soups. Low to medium-low heat.

Pasado: A New Mexico or anaheim chile that has been roasted, peeled, and dried. About 4 inches long and 1 inch wide. Sweet, toasty, dusty flavor. Good for flavoring stews and soups. Medium hot.

Pasilla: Dried chile, also known as "chile negro". About 5 to 7 inches long and 1 inch wide, with dark and wrinkled skin. Sometimes the fresh poblano or the dried ancho and mulato are mistakenly called "pasillas". Deep, rich, almost cocoa-flavor. Used in moles and salsas. Low to medium heat.

Pequin: Tiny dried red chiles. Fiery, sharp, sweet and nutty flavor. Easy to find. Very hot.

(continued on next page)

Poblano: Fresh, dark green and purple-black chile, 4 to 5 inches long and 3 inches wide. Always roasted or cooked. Good for rellenos, or for making into sauces and moles. Rich and meaty. Low heat.

Red Chile Powder: Ground dried red chiles. Varies in quality of flavor and heat.

Sambal Chile: Asian chile. Comes in paste form. Can be found in Asian stores and larger markets. Extremely hot.

Serrano: Fresh green small chile with a clean, sharp heat. Extremely easy to find. Very hot.

Tabasco: Fresh or dried chiles from Louisiana. Used to make Tabasco sauce. Very, very hot.

Thai: Thin, fresh green or dried red chiles, about 1½ inches long and ¼ inch wide. Used in Southeast Asian cooking. Found in specialty stores. Very hot.

Gourmet Tortillas

Exotic and Traditional Tortilla Dishes

by Karen Howarth

This book is lovingly dedicated to Jim, Emily and Sara. Thanks for enjoying and supporting my creativity in the kitchen, for accepting numerous late-evening dinners and for sharing my enthusiasm about living in our tiny cabin next to a beautiful lake.

K. H.

Tortillas

Applesauce Tortillas

I use these tender Applesauce Tortillas for making savory chicken dishes like chimichangas or enchiladas. My kids eat them hot off the griddle, dipped in maple syrup and then sprinkled with cinnamon.

2½ cups white flour
¾ teaspoon salt
1½ teaspoons baking powder
¾ teaspoon cinnamon

- Sift the dry ingredients into a medium bowl.

2 tablespoons butter, softened

- Cut the butter into the flour until the mixture resembles coarse meal.

¾ cup applesauce
water *(as needed)*

- Measure the applesauce in a one-cup, glass measuring cup. Add enough water to the applesauce to equal 7 ounces and stir. Add the liquids to the flour mixture all at once. Mix well.

- Finish making the tortillas by following the directions located on page 9 *(About Making Tortillas)*. Begin with step number 4.

makes eight 8" tortillas

Recommended dishes for using Applesauce Tortillas:

Apple Raspberry Butter & Tortillas (page 120)
Chicken Apple Tortilla Salad (page 89)
Chicken Chimichangas (page 144)
French Toasted Breakfast Tortillas (page 118)
Tortilla Snowflakes (page 82)

Avocado Tortillas

The rich avocado flavor combined with a festive green color make these tortillas unique. They can be rolled out very thin and will remain so while cooking.

2½ cups white flour
1 teaspoon salt
1½ teaspoons baking powder
⅛ teaspoon chile powder

- Sift the dry ingredients into a medium bowl.

1 tablespoon butter, softened

- Cut the butter into the flour until the mixture resembles coarse meal.

1 cup mashed avocado
¼ teaspoon fresh lemon juice
3½ tablespoons water

- In a small bowl, combine mashed avocado, lemon juice and water. Stir. Add the avocado mixture to the flour mixture all at once. Mix well.

- Finish making the tortillas by following the directions located on page 9 *(About Making Tortillas)*. Begin with step number 4. Avocado Tortillas cook a little faster than usual, needing only about 40 seconds per side. Store at room temperature for the first few hours, or refrigerate for longer storage.

makes eight 8" tortillas

Recommended dishes for using Avocado Tortillas:

Garden Vegetable Tortilla Pockets (page 128)
Tortilla Buffet (page 147)
Cheese Enchiladas (page 108)

Beer Tortillas

Imagine ..... soft and aromatic tortillas made with beer! A novelty with guests, these are great for sandwiches and enchiladas, or dipped into your favorite chile.

2½ cups white flour
¾ teaspoon salt
1½ teaspoons baking powder
¼ teaspoon baking soda

- Sift the dry ingredients into a medium bowl.

2 tablespoons butter, softened

- Cut the butter into the flour until the mixture resembles coarse meal.

½ cup plus 2½ tablespoons beer

- Add the beer to the flour mixture all at once. Mix well.
- Finish making the tortillas by following the directions located on page 9 *(About Making Tortillas)*. Begin with step number 4.

makes eight 8" tortillas

Recommended dishes for using Beer Tortillas:

Anaheim Beef Enchiladas (page 106)
Chipotle Chile Taco with Corn (page 152)
Fried Olives (page 74)
Southwestern Onion Soup with Tortillas & Cheese (page 83)
Tortilla Stuffed Chile Peppers with Cashews & Avocado (page 126)

Black Olive & Sour Cream Tortillas

Speckled with black olives and full of flavor, this tortilla is great for enchiladas. It is also wonderful with frijoles and cheese, garnished with several whole black olives. My daughters always request a garnish of five olives ..... one for each fingertip!

2½ cups white flour
¾ teaspoon salt
2 teaspoons baking powder

- Sift the dry ingredients into a medium bowl.

1 tablespoon butter, softened
1 cup finely minced black olives

- Cut the butter into the flour until the mixture resembles coarse meal. Add the olives and mix well.

½ cup sour cream
water *(as needed)*

- Measure the sour cream in a one-cup, glass measuring cup. Add enough water to the sour cream to equal 6½ ounces. Add the sour cream mixture to the flour mixture all at once. Mix well.

- Finish making the tortillas by following the directions located on page 9 *(About Making Tortillas)*. Begin with step number 4. The olives may stick slightly while cooking. If so, use a spatula to loosen the tortillas before turning.

makes eight 8" tortillas

Recommended dishes for using Black Olive & Sour Cream Tortillas:

Chicken Enchiladas (page 109)
Cucumber Tortilla Salad with Parmesan Tomatoes (page 92)
Shredded Beef & Eggplant Enchiladas (page 113)
Steak Fajitas (page 156)

Bran Tortillas

Delicious and earthy in taste, Bran Tortillas make a nutritious and flavorful companion for most soups and salads.

2½	**cups white flour**
1	**teaspoon salt**
1½	**teaspoons baking powder**

• Sift the dry ingredients into a medium bowl.

2	**tablespoons butter, softened**

• Cut the butter into the flour until the mixture resembles coarse meal.

¼	**cup water**
⅛	**cup bran**

• Place the water in a small saucepan over medium heat. Cover and heat until boiling. Add bran. Cook and stir for 1 minute. Remove from heat and cool to room temperature.

2	**tablespoons sour cream**
½	**cup plus 1 tablespoon water**

• Add the sour cream and water to the cooked bran, and stir. Add the bran mixture to the flour mixture all at once. Mix well.

• Finish making the tortillas by following the directions located on page 9 *(About Making Tortillas)*. Begin with step number 4. Cook these tortillas at a slightly higher temperature and for several seconds longer per side than usual.

makes eight 8" tortillas

Recommended dishes for using Bran Tortillas:

Breakfast Burrito (page 104)
Chicken Apple Tortilla Salad (page 89)
Cucumber Tortilla Salad with Parmesan Tomatoes (page 92)

Butter Tortillas

The extra butter in this recipe makes these tortillas especially light and flaky. They are excellent underneath a crisp salad or alongside a large bowl of "hot" chile.

2½ cups white flour
¾ teaspoon salt
2 teaspoons baking powder

- Sift the dry ingredients into a medium bowl.

4 tablespoons butter, softened

- Cut the butter into the flour until the mixture resembles coarse meal.

6½ ounces milk

- Add the milk to the flour mixture all at once. Mix well.
- Finish making the tortillas by following the directions located on page 9 *(About Making Tortillas)*. Begin with step number 4.

makes eight 8" tortillas

Recommended dishes for using Butter Tortillas:

Chilled Asparagus on a Tortilla with Savory Raspberry Sauce (page 90)
Chipotle Chile Taco with Corn (page 152)
Mexican-Style Chicken Steamed Buns (page 140)
Shredded Beef & Eggplant Enchiladas (page 113)

Buttermilk Tortillas

These tortillas have such a soft texture ..... they will melt in your mouth! The addition of buttermilk creates a dough which is smooth and easy to roll, so this is an exceptional tortilla to prepare for your initial experience. Dry buttermilk can be found in the baking section of your grocery store.

2½ cups white flour
¾ teaspoon salt
1½ teaspoons baking powder
2 tablespoons dry buttermilk

- Sift the dry ingredients into a medium bowl.

1½ tablespoons butter, softened

- Cut the butter into the flour until the mixture resembles coarse meal.

6½ ounces water

- Add the water to the flour mixture all at once. Mix well.
- Finish making the tortillas by following the directions located on page 9 *(About Making Tortillas)*. Begin with step number 4. These tortillas should be rolled out quite thin since they tend to contract and become thicker while cooking.

makes eight 8" tortillas

Recommended dishes for using Buttermilk Tortillas:

Chicken & Pistachio Enchiladas (page 110)
Kiwi Chicken Burritos (page 102)
Pizza Quesadillas (page 78)
Tortilla Salad with Buttermilk Caesar Dressing & Homemade Croutons (page 95)

Buttermilk & Potato Tortillas

The combination of buttermilk and potatoes creates a relaxed dough which can be rolled thin, and will remain so when cooked. I use dry buttermilk from the baking section of the grocery store, so that it is always on hand.

2½ cups white flour
¾ teaspoon salt
2 teaspoons baking powder
2½ tablespoons dry buttermilk

- Sift the dry ingredients into a medium bowl.

1½ tablespoons shortening

- Cut the shortening into the flour until the mixture resembles coarse meal.

¼ cup mashed potatoes
water *(as needed)*

- Measure the mashed potatoes in a one-cup, glass measuring cup. Add enough water to the mashed potatoes to equal 7 ounces and stir. Add the potato mixture to the flour mixture all at once. Mix well.

- Finish making the tortillas by following the directions located on page 9 *(About Making Tortillas)*. Begin with step number 4.

makes eight 8" tortillas

Recommended dishes for using Buttermilk & Potato Tortillas:

Breakfast Burrito (page 104)
Cheese Quesadillas (page 76)
Tortilla Poor Boy Sandwich (page 157)
Chicken Chimichangas (page 144)

Campground Tortillas

With a small white gas stove and a lightweight non-stick skillet, you can easily make fresh tortillas while backpacking or camping. It's fun for everyone to make their own, and they are a welcome treat at the end of a long day's hike.

2½ cups white flour
1 teaspoon salt
1 tablespoon baking powder
1½ tablespoons dry buttermilk

- Sift the dry ingredients into a medium bowl.

1½ tablespoons butter, softened

- Cut the butter into the flour until the mixture resembles coarse meal. Place the flour mixture in a large, sealable plastic bag. Remove excess air and seal tightly.

¼ cup white flour, in a small sealable plastic bag
¾ cup water

- At home: Pack the bagged flour-butter mixture, the ¼ cup of flour, a drinking cup with measurements, a camping spoon and a dish towel. *(Don't forget the white gas stove and a non-stick skillet!)*
- At the campsite: Using the sealable plastic bag that contains the flour-butter mixture as a bowl, add the ¾ cup water to the flour mixture all at once. Mix well.
- Gather the dough into a ball and knead briefly inside the plastic bag until the ingredients are well combined. *(The dough should be soft but not sticky.)* Knead in small amounts of the flour *(a teaspoon at a time)* if necessary.
- Divide the dough into 8 equal pieces. Roll each piece into a ball, then flatten slightly. Place the rounds of dough on one half of a clean dish towel and cover them with the other half. Let rest 15 minutes.
- Light the stove and preheat the non-stick skillet over low flame.
- With lightly floured hands, flatten and stretch each piece into a 6" circle. Cook each tortilla on a dry skillet until lightly browned, about 45 seconds per side.

makes eight 6" tortillas

Cheddar Cheese Tortillas

The addition of sharp Cheddar cheese gives this tortilla a colorful appearance and a mild Cheddar flavor that will complement almost any dish you may serve. In our family this is the tortilla that we eat most often!

2½ cups white flour
¾ teaspoon salt
1½ teaspoons baking powder
1 dash cayenne pepper

• Sift the dry ingredients into a medium bowl.

½ tablespoon butter, softened
1 cup finely grated sharp Cheddar cheese

• Cut the butter into the flour until the mixture resembles coarse meal. Add the cheese and stir.

¾ cup plus 1 tablespoon water

• Add the water to the flour mixture all at once. Mix well.

• Finish making the tortillas by following the directions located on page 9 *(About Making Tortillas)*. Begin with step number 4. The Cheddar cheese may stick slightly while cooking. If so, you can use a spatula to loosen the tortillas before turning them over.

makes eight 8" tortillas

Recommended dishes for using Cheddar Cheese Tortillas:

Black Sesame Chicken Appetizers (page 70)
Cheese Burritos with Spicy Frijoles (page 100)
Steak Fajitas (page 156)
Tortilla Buffet (page 147)
Tortilla Eggs Benedict (page 119)
Tortilla Soup (page 88)

"Corn" Tortillas with Caramelized Onion

A unique departure from the traditional masa harina tortilla, this flour tortilla is made with cream style corn and caramelized sweet onion. They are absolutely delicious!

1 tablespoon butter
3½ tablespoons finely minced sweet onion

- In a small saucepan, melt the butter over low heat. Sauté the onion until lightly browned, about 20 minutes. Cool to room temperature.

2½ cups white flour
1 teaspoon salt
1 tablespoon baking powder
⅛ teaspoon dry hot mustard

- Sift the dry ingredients into a medium bowl.

1 tablespoon butter, softened

- Cut the butter into the flour until the mixture resembles coarse meal.

⅔ cup cream style corn, unsalted
¼ cup half & half

- In a small bowl, combine cream style corn, half & half and caramelized onion. Stir. Add cream corn mixture to the flour mixture all at once. Mix well.
- Finish making the tortillas by following the directions located on page 9 *(About Making Tortillas)*. Begin with step number 4.

makes eight 8" tortillas

Recommended dishes for using "Corn" Tortillas with Caramelized Onion:

Creamy Mushroom Soup with Floating Tortillas (page 86)
Sun-Dried Tomato Rice with Hidden Tortillas (page 132)
Taco Salad (page 94)

Corn Tortillas with Cheese & Chives

The combination of white flour with masa harina flour creates a pliable corn tortilla that does not need to be softened by dipping it into hot oil.

1 cup masa harina corn tortilla flour
2 cups white flour
1 teaspoon salt
1½ tablespoons baking powder

- Sift the dry ingredients into a medium bowl.

3 tablespoons butter, softened
½ cup finely grated sharp Cheddar cheese
2½ teaspoons minced fresh chives

- Cut the butter and cheese into the flour until the mixture resembles coarse meal. Add the chives and stir.

1 cup water

- Add the water to the flour mixture all at once. Mix well.
- Finish making the tortillas by following the directions located on page 9 *(About Making Tortillas)*. Begin with step number 4. This corn tortilla is a little stiffer to roll out than flour tortillas, resulting in a less uniform edge. Package the tortillas while they are still hot.

makes eight 8" tortillas

Recommended dishes for using Corn Tortillas with Cheese & Chives:

Cheese Enchiladas (page 108)
Shredded Beef & Eggplant Enchiladas (page 113)
Tortilla Buffet (page 147)

Cottage Cheese Tortillas

Speckled and crispy on the outside, while soft and light on the inside, these tortillas are my solution for using up that little bit of cottage cheese which always seems to be lingering in the refrigerator.

2½ cups white flour
1 teaspoon salt
1½ teaspoons baking powder

- Sift the dry ingredients into a medium bowl.

1 tablespoon butter, softened

- Cut the butter into the flour until the mixture resembles coarse meal.

½ cup cottage cheese *(small curd)*
water *(as needed)*

- Measure the cottage cheese in a one-cup, glass measuring cup. Add enough water to the cottage cheese to equal 7½ ounces and stir. Add the cottage cheese mixture to the flour mixture all at once. Mix well.

- Finish making the tortillas by following the directions located on page 9 *(About Making Tortillas)*. Begin with step number 4. The cottage cheese may stick slightly while cooking. If so, use a spatula to loosen the tortillas before turning them over.

makes eight 8" tortillas

Recommended dishes for using Cottage Cheese Tortillas:

Chilled Asparagus on a Tortilla with Savory Raspberry Sauce (page 90)
Creamy Mushroom Soup with Floating Tortillas (page 86)
Grilled Skewers of Filet Mignon with a Spirited Horseradish Sauce (page 154)
Marinated Beef Burritos (page 105)
Mexican-Style Chicken Steamed Buns (page 140)
Shredded Beef Tortilla Pockets (page 150)
Vegetable Frittata Wrapped in Tortillas (page 122)

Cream Cheese Tortillas

Cream Cheese Tortillas are especially wonderful because of their rich flavor and delicate texture. On special occasions I serve them for breakfast, hot off the skillet, accompanied with sweet orange butter. These tortillas are at their best when eaten the same day they are prepared.

2½ cups white flour
¾ teaspoon salt
1½ teaspoons baking powder

- Sift the dry ingredients into a medium bowl.

1 tablespoon butter, softened
2 ounces cream cheese, softened

- Cut the butter and cream cheese into the flour until the mixture resembles coarse meal.

5½ ounces water

- Add the water to the flour mixture all at once. Mix well.
- Finish making the tortillas by following the directions located on page 9 *(About Making Tortillas)*. Begin with step number 4.

makes eight 8" tortillas

Recommended dishes for using Cream Cheese Tortillas:

Apricot Prawns with Tortillas (page 136)
French Toasted Breakfast Tortillas (page 118)
New York Steak Enchiladas (page 114)
Orange Chicken Tortilla Pockets with Raisins (page 142)
Taco Salad (page 94)

Jalapeño Tortillas

Jalapeño Tortillas are mildly spiced with hot chiles, lemon balm and fresh chives. The addition of fresh buttermilk gives them a feathery, cake-like texture. If you like your food hot and spicy, add another teaspoon of jalapeño chile pepper.

1 teaspoon very finely minced jalapeño chile pepper, seeds and membrane removed
1 cup fresh buttermilk

- Stir the jalapeño chile pepper into the buttermilk. Let stand at room temperature for 10 minutes.

2½ cups white flour
1 teaspoon salt
1½ tablespoons baking powder

- Sift the dry ingredients into a medium bowl.

1 tablespoon butter, softened
1½ teaspoons finely minced fresh lemon balm
2 teaspoons finely minced fresh chives

- Cut the butter into the flour until the mixture resembles coarse meal. Add the lemon balm and minced chives. Stir.
- Add the buttermilk mixture to the flour mixture all at once. Mix well.
- Finish making the tortillas by following the directions located on page 9 *(About Making Tortillas)*. Begin with step number 4.

makes eight 8" tortillas

Recommended dishes for using Jalapeño Tortillas:

Cheese Enchiladas (page 108)
Kiwi Chicken Burritos (page 102)
Marinated Halibut Tacos (page 146)
New York Steak Enchiladas (page 114)
Shredded Beef & Eggplant Enchiladas (page 113)
Tortilla Soup (page 88)

Lavender Tortillas with Garlic Chives

The sweet taste of lavender combined with the spiciness of ground jalapeño chile pepper and fresh garlic chives make this tortilla both exotic and memorable. Try miniature one-inch tortillas, by making only half of this recipe and then dividing the dough into 36 equal pieces.

2½	**cups white flour**
1	**teaspoon salt**
1	**tablespoon baking powder**

- Sift the dry ingredients into a medium bowl.

2	**tablespoons butter, softened**
½	**teaspoon minced fresh lavender**
2	**tablespoons minced fresh garlic chives**
¼	**teaspoon ground jalapeño chile pepper**

- Cut the butter into the flour until the mixture resembles coarse meal. Add the lavender, garlic chives and ground jalapeño chile pepper. Mix well.

7	**ounces water**

- Add the water to the flour mixture all at once. Mix well.
- Finish making the tortillas by following the directions located on page 9 *(About Making Tortillas)*. Begin with step number 4.

makes eight 8" tortillas

Recommended dishes for using Lavender Tortillas with Garlic Chives:

Anaheim Beef Enchiladas (page 106)
Black Sesame Chicken Appetizers (page 70)
Cheese Enchiladas (page 108)
Creamy Mushroom Soup with Floating Tortillas (page 86)

Lemon Spinach Tortillas

These soft tortillas have the crispness of fresh spinach and the tangy zest of lemon. Both of my children love to eat them but I never reveal that spinach is the "secret" ingredient.

2½ cups white flour
1⅛ teaspoons salt
1 tablespoon baking powder
¼ teaspoon freshly grated lemon zest

- Sift the dry ingredients into a medium bowl. Add the grated lemon zest and stir.

1 tablespoon butter, softened
⅓ cup finely minced fresh spinach, ribs removed

- Cut the butter into the flour until the mixture resembles coarse meal. Add the spinach to the flour mixture and stir.

¾ cup water

- Add the water to the flour mixture all at once. Mix well.
- Finish making the tortillas by following the directions located on page 9 *(About Making Tortillas)*. Begin with step number 4.

makes eight 8" tortillas

Recommended dishes for using Lemon Spinach Tortillas:

Asiago Fettucine (page 135)
Steak Fajitas (page 156)
Tortilla Salad with Buttermilk Caesar Dressing & Homemade Croutons (page 95)

Oatmeal Tortillas

The subtle oatmeal flavor and chewy texture are what set this tortilla apart from all others. They are wonderful for breakfast when served with eggs, instead of toast. Young people enjoy them filled with peanut butter and jelly, rolled up and cut into pinwheels. I've learned that the addition of a fancy toothpick goes a long way with children!

2½ cups white flour
1 teaspoon salt
1¾ teaspoons baking powder

- Sift the dry ingredients into a medium bowl.

2 tablespoons butter, softened

- Cut the butter into the flour until the mixture resembles coarse meal.

½ cup cooked oatmeal
5 ounces water

- In a small bowl, combine the cooked oatmeal and water. Add the oatmeal mixture to the flour mixture all at once. Mix well.
- Finish making the tortillas by following the directions located on page 9 *(About Making Tortillas)*. Begin with step number 4. Cook these tortillas at a slightly higher temperature and for several seconds longer per side than usual.

makes eight 8" tortillas

Recommended dishes for using Oatmeal Tortillas:

Apple Raspberry Butter & Tortillas (page 120)
Breakfast Burrito (page 104)
Sunny-Side Up Fried Rice Over Tortillas (page 130)

Orange Tortillas with Montmorency Cherries

This recipe is made with dried Montmorency cherries, which we pick fresh here in Washington state, and then dry. The cherries are the size of a raisin, with a deep red color and a slightly tart, rich cherry flavor. Try these tortillas for breakfast with sweet butter and orange marmalade.

2½ cups white flour
1 teaspoon salt
4 teaspoons baking powder
1 tablespoon sugar
1 teaspoon freshly grated orange zest

- Sift the dry ingredients into a medium bowl. Add the grated orange zest and stir.

2 tablespoons butter, softened
1 tablespoon minced dried Montmorency cherries *(unsweetened)*

- Cut the butter into the flour until the mixture resembles coarse meal. Add the dried cherries and stir.

¾ cup water

- Add the water to the flour mixture all at once. Mix well.
- Finish making the tortillas by following the directions located on page 9 *(About Making Tortillas)*. Begin with step number 4.

makes eight 8" tortillas

Recommended dishes for using Orange Tortillas with Montmorency Cherries:

Chicken & Pistachio Enchiladas (page 110)
French Toasted Breakfast Tortillas (page 118)
Tortilla Snowflakes (page 82)

Parmesan Cheese Tortillas

The addition of freshly grated Parmesan cheese produces a delightful, cheesy tortilla with an incredible texture. I find them to be a perfect companion for most main dishes.

2½ cups white flour
½ teaspoon salt
1½ teaspoons baking powder
1 dash cayenne pepper

- Sift the dry ingredients into a medium bowl.

2 tablespoons butter, softened
⅔ cup freshly grated Parmesan cheese

- Cut the butter into the flour until the mixture resembles coarse meal. Add the cheese and stir.

¾ cup plus 2 tablespoons water

- Add the water to the flour mixture all at once. Mix well.
- Finish making the tortillas by following the directions located on page 9 *(About Making Tortillas)*. Begin with step number 4. The Parmesan cheese may stick while cooking. If so, use a spatula to loosen the tortillas before turning them over.

makes eight 8" tortillas

Recommended dishes for using Parmesan Cheese Tortillas:

Chicken Apple Tortilla Salad (page 89)
Chicken Chimichangas (page 144)
Orange Chicken Tortilla Pockets with Raisins (page 142)
Tortilla Salad with Buttermilk Caesar Dressing & Homemade Croutons (page 95)

Potato Tortillas

I use up small amounts of left over mashed potatoes to create these incredibly thick and chewy tortillas. Usually served for breakfast, they are filled with various egg concoctions, depending on the herbs available for harvest in the garden and the cook's mood of the day.

2½ cups white flour
1 teaspoon salt
1½ teaspoons baking powder

- Sift the dry ingredients into a medium bowl.

1½ tablespoons butter, softened

- Cut the butter into the flour until the mixture resembles coarse meal.

½ cup mashed potatoes
water *(as needed)*

- Measure the mashed potatoes in a one-cup, glass measuring cup. Add enough water to the mashed potatoes to equal 7 ounces and stir. Add the potato mixture to the flour mixture all at once. Mix well.

- Finish making the tortillas by following the directions located on page 9 *(About Making Tortillas)*. Begin with step number 4.

makes eight 8" tortillas

Recommended dishes for using Potato Tortillas:

Garden Vegetable Tortilla Pockets (page 128)
Grilled Skewers of Filet Mignon with a Spirited Horseradish Sauce (page 154)
Tortilla Eggs Benedict (page 119)

Potato & Yogurt Tortillas

The combination of mashed potatoes and creamy plain yogurt gives this tortilla a satisfying chewy texture, with a longer shelf life than others.

2½ cups white flour
1 teaspoon salt
1½ teaspoons baking powder

- Sift the dry ingredients into a medium bowl.

1½ tablespoons butter, softened

- Cut the butter into the flour until the mixture resembles coarse meal.

¼ cup plain yogurt
¼ cup mashed potatoes
water *(as needed)*

- Combine the yogurt and mashed potatoes in a one-cup, glass measuring cup. Add enough water to the yogurt mixture to equal 7 ounces and stir. Add the yogurt mixture to the flour mixture all at once. Mix well.

- Finish making the tortillas by following the directions located on page 9 *(About Making Tortillas)*. Begin with step number 4.

makes eight 8" tortillas

Recommended dishes for using Potato & Yogurt Tortillas:

Chicken & Chive Filled Tortillas with Cream Sauce (page 138)
Chicken Enchiladas (page 109)
Shredded Beef Tortilla Pockets (page 150)

Red Bell Pepper Tortillas

These are attractive tortillas with a vibrant red color and a sweet bell pepper taste. If you want to be really creative, substitute half of the red pepper with yellow or orange.

2 tablespoons butter
2½ tablespoons minced red bell pepper

- Melt butter in a small saucepan over low heat. Sauté red bell pepper until tender, about 10 minutes. Cool to room temperature.

2½ cups white flour
1 teaspoon salt
1½ tablespoons baking powder

- Sift the dry ingredients into a medium bowl.

1 tablespoon butter, softened

- Cut the butter into the flour until the mixture resembles coarse meal. Add the sautéed red bell pepper and mix well.

6½ ounces milk
½ teaspoon fresh lemon juice

- Measure the milk in a one-cup, glass measuring cup. Add the lemon juice to the milk. Let sit for 5 minutes. Add the milk mixture to the flour mixture all at once. Mix well.

- Finish making the tortillas by following the directions located on page 9 *(About Making Tortillas)*. Begin with step number 4.

makes eight 8" tortillas

(continued on next page)

Recommended dishes for using Red Bell Pepper Tortillas:

Apricot Prawns with Tortillas (page 136)
Cheese Quesadillas (page 76)
Chicken & Chive Filled Tortillas with Cream Sauce (page 138)
Chicken Enchiladas (page 109)
Cucumber Tortilla Salad with Parmesan Tomatoes (page 92)
Sunny-Side Up Fried Rice Over Tortillas (page 130)

Risen (Yeast) Tortillas

This "hybrid" combines the chewy texture and flattened shape of a tortilla with the flavor and personality of a homestyle yeast bread. By far, it is the most requested tortilla that I make. Prepare them when your kitchen is warm, and allow plenty of time for the dough to rise.

2½ cups white flour
1 teaspoon salt
1 teaspoon baking powder
1 dash cayenne pepper
2 teaspoons dry yeast

- Sift the dry ingredients *(except the yeast)* into a medium bowl. Add the yeast and stir.

2 tablespoons butter, softened

- Cut the butter into the flour until the mixture resembles coarse meal.

¼ teaspoon fresh lemon juice
7 ounces milk

- Add the lemon juice to the milk and stir. Let sit for 5 minutes. Add the milk mixture to the flour mixture all at once. Mix well.
- Gather the dough into a ball and knead 8 to 10 minutes, until smooth and elastic. Add small amounts of flour while kneading to prevent dough from sticking. Place the kneaded dough in a medium, buttered bowl and cover with a clean dish towel. Let rise until double in size, about 1½ to 2 hours. *(Remember, a yeast dough will rise much faster in a warm kitchen than it will in a cool kitchen.)* Punch down the dough and knead briefly.
- Finish making the tortillas by following the directions located on page 10 *(About Making Tortillas)*. Begin with step number 5.

makes eight 8" tortillas

(continued on next page)

Recommended dishes for using Risen (Yeast) Tortillas:

Cheese Burritos with Spicy Frijoles (page 100)
Chicken Chimichangas (page 144)
Shredded Beef Tortilla Pockets (page 150)
Southwestern Onion Soup with Tortillas & Cheese (page 83)
Tiny Greek Tortilla "Pizzas" (page 148)
Tortilla Eggs Benedict (page 119)

Romano Cheese & Chive Tortillas

I make these tortillas in early summer when the herbs in our garden are young and tender. You will love the way the aroma of chives and Romano cheese fills your kitchen.

2½ cups white flour
¾ teaspoon salt
1½ tablespoons baking powder
1 dash white pepper

- Sift the dry ingredients into a medium bowl.

2 tablespoons butter, softened
1 tablespoon freshly grated Romano cheese
¼ cup finely minced fresh chives

- Cut the butter into the flour until the mixture resembles coarse meal. Add the Romano cheese and minced chives. Stir.

7 ounces milk

- Add the milk to the flour mixture all at once. Mix well.
- Finish making the tortillas by following the directions located on page 9 *(About Making Tortillas)*. Begin with step number 4.

makes eight 8" tortillas

Recommended dishes for using Romano Cheese & Chive Tortillas:

Cheese Quesadillas (page 76)
Chicken & Zucchini Enchiladas (page 112)
Fried Olives (page 74)
Grilled Skewers of Filet Mignon with a Spirited Horseradish Sauce (page 154)
Marinated Halibut Tacos (page 146)
Pizza Quesadillas (page 78)

Scallion Tortillas

A showy presentation joined with the sweet pungent flavor of green scallions makes this tortilla stand apart from the others.

2½	**cups white flour**
¾	**teaspoon salt**
1½	**teaspoons baking powder**

• Sift the dry ingredients into a medium bowl.

1	**tablespoon butter, softened**

• Cut the butter into the flour until the mixture resembles coarse meal.

⅓	**cup finely minced scallions**
7	**ounces water**

• Stir the scallions into the flour mixture. Add the water to the flour mixture all at once. Mix well.

• Finish making the tortillas by following the directions located on page 9 *(About Making Tortillas)*. Begin with step number 4.

makes eight 8" tortillas

Recommended dishes for using Scallion Tortillas:

Chipotle Chile Taco with Corn (page 152)
Garden Vegetable Tortilla Pockets (page 128)
Marinated Beef Burritos (page 105)
Vegetable Frittata Wrapped in Tortillas (page 122)

Sour Cream Tortillas

Thick and rich in substance, these spectacular tortillas have a surprisingly light texture which creates a delightful contrast!

2½ cups white flour
¾ teaspoon salt
1½ teaspoons baking powder

- Sift the dry ingredients into a medium bowl.

1½ tablespoons butter, softened

- Cut the butter into the flour until the mixture resembles coarse meal.

½ cup sour cream
2 tablespoons milk
water *(as needed)*

- Measure the sour cream in a one-cup, glass measuring cup. Add the milk and stir. Add enough water to the sour cream mixture to equal 7½ ounces. Mix well.
- Add the sour cream mixture to the flour mixture all at once. Mix well.
- Finish making the tortillas by following the directions located on page 9 *(About Making Tortillas)*. Begin with step number 4. The dough will initially stick to your fingers and is a little messy to work with. Don't worry, this is normal. These tortillas will require a little longer cooking time, at a slightly lower temperature. Cook until well browned.

makes eight 8" tortillas

Recommended dishes for using Sour Cream Tortillas:

Anaheim Beef Enchiladas (page 106)
Apricot Prawns with Tortillas (page 136)
Fried Olives (page 74)
Garden Vegetable Tortilla Pockets (page 128)
Tortilla Stuffed Chile Peppers with Cashews & Avocado (page 126)

Sour Cream & Potato Tortillas

This satiny smooth dough is very easy to roll and creates a nice, light textured tortilla when cooked. I make these tortillas when I find small amounts of mashed potatoes, remaining unnoticed, in the refrigerator.

2½ cups white flour
1 teaspoon salt
2 teaspoons baking powder

- Sift the dry ingredients into a medium bowl.

1½ tablespoons butter, softened

- Cut the butter into the flour until the mixture resembles coarse meal.

¼ cup mashed potatoes
¼ cup sour cream
½ cup minus 1 tablespoon water

- In a small bowl, combine mashed potatoes, sour cream and water. Stir. Add the potato mixture to the flour mixture all at once. Mix well.
- Finish making the tortillas by following the directions located on page 9 *(About Making Tortillas)*. Begin with step number 4.

makes eight 8" tortillas

Recommended dishes for using Sour Cream & Potato Tortillas:

Chilled Asparagus on a Tortilla with Savory Raspberry Sauce (page 90)
Cheese Burritos with Spicy Frijoles (page 100)
Vegetable Frittata Wrapped in Tortillas (page 122)

Sourdough Tortillas

This is a thin and chewy tortilla, with the wonderful tang of sourdough. Because the sourdough starter takes at least 3 days to mature, plan on making this recipe well in advance.

1¾ cups white flour
1 teaspoon salt
2 teaspoons baking powder

- Sift the dry ingredients into a medium bowl.

1½ tablespoons butter, softened

- Cut the butter into the flour until the mixture resembles coarse meal.

1 cup Sourdough Starter *(recipe page 168),* **room temperature**

- Add the Sourdough Starter to the flour mixture all at once. Mix well.
- Finish making the tortillas by following the directions located on page 9 *(About Making Tortillas)*. Begin with step number 4.

makes eight 8" tortillas

Recommended dishes for using Sourdough Tortillas:

Chicken & Chive Filled Tortillas with Cream Sauce (page 138)
Marinated Beef Burritos (page 105)
Marinated Halibut Tacos (page 146)
Tiny Greek Tortilla "Pizzas" (page 148)
Tortilla Poor Boy Sandwich (page 157)

Sun-Dried Tomato Tortillas

I love these tortillas for both their colorful appearance and their sweet, slightly tangy sun-dried tomato taste.

2 tablespoons butter
6 sun-dried tomatoes, finely minced

- Heat butter in a small pan until hot. Add tomatoes and remove from heat. Let sit for 15 minutes.

2½ cups white flour
¾ teaspoon salt
1½ teaspoons baking powder

- Sift the dry ingredients into a medium bowl.

2 tablespoons butter, softened

- Cut the butter into the flour until the mixture resembles coarse meal.

7½ ounces milk

- Stir tomato mixture into flour. Add the milk to the flour mixture all at once. Mix well.
- Finish making the tortillas by following the directions located on page 9 *(About Making Tortillas)*. Begin with step number 4.

makes eight 8" tortillas

Recommended dishes for using Sun-Dried Tomato Tortillas:

Asiago Fettucine (page 135)
Cheese Enchiladas (page 108)
Chicken & Zucchini Enchiladas (page 112)
Pizza Quesadillas (page 78)

Steamed Tortillas

Steamed tortillas are unlike any other tortilla in this book. Glossy in appearance, they have a soft, chewy texture similar to a slice of bread without the crust. For an outstanding contrast in textures, try them underneath a crisp green salad.

2½ cups white flour
1 teaspoon salt
1 tablespoon baking powder
2 dashes cayenne pepper

- Sift the dry ingredients into a medium bowl.

2 teaspoons butter, softened
1 tablespoon finely minced fresh chives

- Cut the butter into the flour until the mixture resembles coarse meal. Add the chives and stir.

½ cup half & half
water *(as needed)*

- Measure the half & half in a one-cup, glass measuring cup. Add enough water to the half & half to equal 7 ounces and stir.
- Add the liquids to the flour mixture all at once. Mix well. Gather the dough into a ball and knead briefly until the ingredients are well combined. The dough should be soft but not sticky.
- Divide the dough into 8 equal pieces. In the palm of your hand, roll each piece into a ball then flatten slightly. Place the rounds of dough on one half of a clean dish towel and cover them with the other half. Let rest 10 minutes.

water *(as needed)*
1 corn husk *(for steaming)*

- Preheat a covered 8" skillet over medium heat, containing a flat vegetable steamer and ½" depth of water, until hot and steamy. Line the steamer with a corn husk to prevent the tortillas from sticking.

(continued on next page)

- On a lightly floured board, roll out 1 piece into a 5" circle. Place the tortilla on the corn husk, cover and steam for 2 minutes. Using a spatula, turn the tortilla over and steam, covered, another 2 minutes. Remove the cooked tortilla and place on a wire rack to cool. Continue rolling and steaming the remaining 7 tortillas. *(Be sure to check the water level in the skillet often, adding hot water if necessary.)*
- Package the cooled tortillas in a sealed plastic bag and store at room temperature.

makes eight 5" tortillas

Recommended dishes for using Steamed Tortillas:

Soft Tostada (page 133)
Steamed Botana (page 80)

Traditional Flour Tortillas

This book would not be complete without a recipe for the most common tortilla known to Americans. Requiring only a few basic ingredients which can be found in most kitchens, they are a perfect "spur of the moment" treat.

2½ cups white flour
1 teaspoon salt
1½ teaspoons baking powder

• Sift the dry ingredients into a medium bowl.

2 tablespoons shortening

• Cut the shortening into the flour until the mixture resembles coarse meal.

¾ cup water

• Add the water to the flour mixture all at once. Mix well.

• Finish making the tortillas by following the directions located on page 9 *(About Making Tortillas)*. Begin with step number 4.

makes eight 8" tortillas

Recommended dishes for using Traditional Flour Tortillas:

Apple Raspberry Butter & Tortillas (page 120)
Asiago Fettucine (page 135)
Black Sesame Chicken Appetizers (page 70)
Sunny-Side Up Fried Rice Over Tortillas (page 130)
Tortilla Snowflakes (page 82)
Tortilla Soup (page 88)
Tortilla Stuffed Chile Peppers with Cashews & Avocado (page 126)

Whole Wheat Tortillas

Whole wheat flour and white flour come together to create a finely textured tortilla with a delicious nutty flavor. Serve these for a healthy way to enhance your favorite sandwiches and salads.

3/4 cup whole wheat flour
1 3/4 cups white flour
3/4 teaspoon salt
2 teaspoons baking powder

- Sift the dry ingredients into a medium bowl.

1 1/2 tablespoons shortening

- Cut the shortening into the flour until the mixture resembles coarse meal.

3/4 cup plus 2 tablespoons water

- Add the water to the flour mixture all at once. Mix well.
- Finish making the tortillas by following the directions located on page 9 *(About Making Tortillas)*. Begin with step number 4. Cook these tortillas at a slightly higher temperature and for several seconds less per side than usual. They are most tender when they are removed from the heat before they are allowed to brown.

makes eight 8" tortillas

Recommended dishes for using Whole Wheat Tortillas:

Chicken & Pistachio Enchiladas (page 110)
Mexican-Style Chicken Steamed Buns (page 140)
Sun-Dried Tomato Rice with Hidden Tortillas (page 132)

Yogurt Tortillas

Because this dough is very easy to roll, Yogurt Tortillas are an excellent choice for your first experience at making homemade tortillas. They will remain soft and moist after several days of storage, although I predict they won't be around that long!

2½ cups white flour
1 teaspoon salt
1½ teaspoons baking powder

- Sift the dry ingredients into a medium bowl.

1½ tablespoons butter, softened

- Cut the butter into the flour until the mixture resembles coarse meal.

½ cup plain yogurt
water *(as needed)*

- Measure the yogurt in a one-cup, glass measuring cup. Add enough water to the yogurt to equal 7 ounces and stir. Add the yogurt mixture to the flour mixture all at once. Mix well.

- Finish making the tortillas by following the directions located on page 9 *(About Making Tortillas)*. Begin with step number 4.

makes eight 8" tortillas

Recommended dishes for using Yogurt Tortillas:

Chicken & Zucchini Enchiladas (page 112)
New York Steak Enchiladas (page 114)
Orange Chicken Tortilla Pockets with Raisins (page 142)
Southwestern Onion Soup with Tortillas & Cheese (page 83)
Sun-Dried Tomato Rice with Hidden Tortillas (page 132)

Yogurt Soda Tortillas

Yogurt Soda Tortillas are an excellent change of pace from dinner rolls or sliced bread for sandwiches. The baking soda gives them a soft, cake-like texture.

2½ cups white flour
¾ teaspoon salt
1¼ teaspoons baking powder
⅓ teaspoon baking soda

- Sift the dry ingredients into a medium bowl.

1½ tablespoons butter, softened

- Cut the butter into the flour until the mixture resembles coarse meal.

½ cup plain yogurt
water *(as needed)*

- Measure the yogurt in a one-cup, glass measuring cup. Add enough water to the yogurt to equal 7 ounces and stir. Add the yogurt mixture to the flour mixture all at once. Mix well.

- Finish making the tortillas by following the directions located on page 9 *(About Making Tortillas)*. Begin with step number 4.

makes eight 8" tortillas

Recommended dishes for using Yogurt Soda Tortillas:

Cucumber Tortilla Salad with Parmesan Tomatoes (page 92)
Kiwi Chicken Burritos (page 102)
Tortilla Poor Boy Sandwich (page 157)

Appetizers, Soups & Salads

Black Sesame Chicken Appetizers

A close friend of mine with an Asian heritage was the inspiration for this recipe. Similar to Chinese dimsums and pot stickers, these delicious steamed appetizers can be made in advance and then reheated in the microwave.

1	**cup cooked and finely shredded chicken, skin removed**
½	**cup finely grated sharp Cheddar cheese**
1	**scallion, finely sliced**
½	**teaspoon black sesame seeds**
½	**teaspoon dried chervil**
1	**dash paprika**
1	**dash salt**
2	**dashes black pepper**

- In a small bowl, combine shredded chicken, Cheddar cheese and sliced scallion. Add the sesame seeds and spices. Mix well. Cover and refrigerate until ready for use.

dough for Traditional Flour Tortillas *(recipe page 64),* **or Lavender Tortillas with Garlic Chives** *(recipe page 45),* **or Cheddar Cheese Tortillas** *(recipe page 39)*

- Divide the dough into 16 balls. Flatten each ball into a 2" circle. Let rest 10 minutes.

	water *(as needed)*
1	**corn husk** *(for steaming)*

- Using your thumb, make a depression in the center of 1 piece of dough. Place 1 tablespoon of the filling in the depression and fold in half. Pinch well to seal edges and place on a sheet of wax paper. Continue with the remaining 15 pieces of dough.

- Preheat oven to 200°.

(continued on next page)

- Preheat a covered 8" skillet over medium heat, containing a flat vegetable steamer and ½" depth of water, until hot and steamy. Line the steamer with the corn husk to prevent the tortillas from sticking.

- Steam 4 of the filled tortillas in the preheated skillet, covered, for 2 minutes. Using a spatula, carefully turn each tortilla over. Replace the cover and continue to steam for another 2 minutes. Remove cooked tortillas and place them on a wire rack in the oven, to keep warm. Continue steaming, 4 at a time, with the remaining 12 filled tortillas. *(Be sure to check the water level in the skillet often, adding hot water if necessary.)*

½ **cup Brown Sauce II** *(recipe page 166),* **warmed**
½ **cup sour cream**
½ **cup salsa** *(your favorite)*

- Serve the warm, filled tortillas, accompanied by small bowls of Brown Sauce II, sour cream and your favorite salsa.

makes 16

Fresh Spinach Appetizers in Cheddar Cheese Patty Shells

This is an adaptation of a popular Pacific Northwest potluck appetizer dish, served in petite Cheddar Cheese Patty Shells. Garnished with Gruyere cheese and crisp bacon, it is spectacular in its presentation. I prepare the spinach filling in advance and fill the patty shells just prior to serving.

Fresh Spinach Appetizers

- **2 tablespoons butter**
- **¼ cup finely minced onion**
- **4 cups coarsely chopped fresh spinach, washed and dried, stems removed**

• Melt butter in a medium skillet. Sauté onion over medium-low heat until translucent, about 10 minutes. Add spinach and sauté until wilted, about 2 to 3 minutes.

- **½ cup mayonnaise**
- **½ cup sour cream**
- **½ cup fresh bread crumbs**
- **½ teaspoon fresh lime juice**
- **salt and black pepper** *(to taste)*

• Place sautéed spinach, mayonnaise, sour cream, bread crumbs and lime juice in a small bowl. Season with salt and black pepper. Cover and refrigerate until ready to serve.

- **36 Cheddar Cheese Patty Shells** *(recipe page 73)*
- **½ cup finely grated Gruyere cheese**
- **¼ cup crisp bacon, crumbled**

• Fill each patty shell with about 1½ teaspoons of the chilled spinach mixture. Sprinkle each with a little grated Gruyere cheese and crumbled bacon.

makes 36

Cheddar Cheese Patty Shells

2½ cups white flour
¾ teaspoon salt
1½ teaspoons baking powder

- Sift the dry ingredients into a medium bowl.

½ tablespoon butter, softened
1 cup finely grated extra sharp Cheddar cheese

- Cut the butter into the flour until the mixture resembles coarse meal. Add the cheese and mix well.

¾ cup plus 1 tablespoon water

- Add the water to the flour mixture all at once. Mix well. Gather the dough into a ball and knead briefly until the ingredients are well combined. Divide in half.
- On a lightly floured board, roll out half of the dough into a 10" x 18" rectangle. Let rest 10 minutes.
- Preheat oven to 375°.
- Using a 2¾" cookie cutter, cut out as many circles as possible. *(Do not reroll the dough that is left over, as this will result in tough patty shells.)* Place 1 circle in each ungreased muffin cup. Take care to place the circles over the cups evenly before pushing the dough to the bottom with your fingers. Prick each shell several times with a fork before baking.
- Bake unfilled shells for 7 to 8 minutes, or until puffy but not browned.
- Remove immediately from pan, place on paper towels and cool slightly. Package them in a plastic bag while still warm. Store at room temperature or freeze them for later use.

Note: These patty shells can be filled with many different things. Try cream cheese and shrimp, mixed fruit, pasta salad ..... or whatever your imagination leads you to!

makes 36 to 40

Fried Olives

Fried Olives are as much fun to make as they are to eat! The black olives are filled with cream cheese and minced yellow chile pepper, then encased in tortilla dough and fried until crisp and golden brown.

1½ ounces cream cheese, softened
¾ teaspoon finely minced shallot
1 tablespoon minced yellow chile pepper, seeds and membrane removed
1 dash paprika
1 dash black pepper

- In a very small bowl, combine cream cheese, shallot, chile pepper and spices. Refrigerate until chilled, about 30 minutes.

40 large pitted black olives

- Place olives on a paper towel and pat to dry. Fill each olive with a small amount of the cream cheese mixture.

dough for Romano Cheese & Chive Tortillas *(recipe page 56),* **or Beer Tortillas** *(recipe page 32),* **or Sour Cream Tortillas** *(recipe page 58)*

- Divide dough into 40 balls and flatten each slightly. Place 1 olive in the center of each piece of dough. Stretch the dough gently around the olive and pinch well to seal.

- Preheat oven to 200°.

vegetable oil *(as needed)*

- Place vegetable oil, ½" deep, in an 8" skillet. Preheat oil over medium heat until very hot, but not smoking. Deep-fry 10 olives in the hot oil until golden brown, turning only once, about 45 seconds per side. Place the fried olives in an oven-proof baking dish lined with paper towels. Keep warm in the oven until ready to serve. Continue, 10 at a time, with the remaining 30 olives.

(continued on next page)

- 3⁄4 **cup Guacamole** *(recipe page 93)*
- 3⁄4 **cup sour cream**
- 3⁄4 **cup salsa** *(your favorite)*

• Serve the olives immediately with Guacamole, sour cream and your favorite salsa.

makes 40

Cheese Quesadillas

These quesadillas differ from the traditional because they are filled with cheese before cooking the tortillas, instead of after, which results in a very soft and luscious texture.

dough for Buttermilk & Potato Tortillas *(recipe page 37),* **or Romano Cheese & Chive Tortillas** *(recipe page 56),* **or Red Bell Pepper Tortillas** *(recipe page 52)*

- Divide the dough into 10 pieces. Let rest 15 minutes.

1 cup finely grated sharp Cheddar cheese
⅔ cup finely grated Mozzarella cheese

- Combine cheeses in a medium bowl and mix well.
- On a lightly floured board, roll out 2 pieces of dough into 8" circles. Place ⅓ cup cheese evenly over 1 of the tortillas, staying ½" from the edge. Place the other rolled tortilla on top of the cheese. Crimp the edge, halfway around the tortilla, by pressing firmly with fingertips. Using a rolling pin, start from the crimped side and gently roll over the top tortilla to remove any air bubbles. Crimp the remaining edge.
- Preheat a large skillet over medium-low heat.
- Cook the tortilla on a dry skillet until lightly browned, about 1½ minutes per side, turning only once. Continue to prepare the remaining 8 pieces of dough in the same manner.
- Stack the cooked tortillas on a wire rack to cool slightly.

salsa *(your favorite)*

- Cut each quesadilla into 8 wedges and serve with your favorite salsa.

makes 40 wedges

Nacho Appetizers

As popular with kids as they are with adults, these "easy to eat" nachos are always quick to disappear at a party. No matter how many I make, there never seems to be enough!

2 cups Spicy Frijoles *(recipe page 101),* **heated**
36 Cheddar Cheese Patty Shells *(recipe page 73)*

- Place about 1 teaspoon of Spicy Frijoles in each patty shell.

4 ounces Cheddar cheese, cut into 36 cubes, ¼" square
10 pitted black olives, thinly sliced
1 jalapeño chile pepper, seeds and membrane removed, very finely minced
sour cream *(as needed)*
salsa *(your favorite)*

- Preheat oven to broil.
- Top each of the filled patty shells with 1 cube of Cheddar cheese. Place several black olives on top of half the patty shells. Top the rest of the patty shells with the minced jalapeño chile pepper. Place on a baking sheet.
- Broil on the top rack for 2 to 3 minutes, or until lightly browned.
- Serve warm with sour cream and your favorite salsa.

makes 36

Pizza Quesadillas with Basil Parmesan Tomato Sauce

Two stacked tortillas with a center of cheese are topped with a spicy pizza sauce and black olives, then cut into wedges to make a fun and festive appetizer for parties. Use the sauce for other pizzas or on fresh pasta.

Pizza Quesadillas

1¼ **cups grated Mozzarella cheese**
1¼ **cups grated Provolone cheese**
10 **Romano Cheese & Chive Tortillas** *(recipe page 56),* **Sun-Dried Tomato Tortillas** *(recipe page 61),* **or Buttermilk Tortillas** *(recipe page 36)*

- Preheat oven to broil.
- In a medium bowl, combine the cheeses.
- Place 5 tortillas on 2 ungreased baking sheets. Top each tortilla with ¼ cup of the combined cheeses, reserving the rest. Broil until cheese is melted but not browned. Remove from oven. *(Leave the broiler on.)* Place 1 remaining tortilla on top of each.

1 **cup Basil Parmesan Tomato Sauce** *(recipe page 79),* **heated**
½ **cup thinly sliced black olives**

- Top each quesadilla with 3 tablespoons of the Basil Parmesan Tomato Sauce. Sprinkle ¼ cup of the remaining cheese over each and top with sliced black olives. Broil until cheese is melted and bubbly.

freshly grated Parmesan cheese *(as needed)*
crushed red pepper *(as needed)*

- Cut each tortilla into 8 triangles. Serve with freshly grated Parmesan cheese and crushed red pepper.

makes 40 wedges

Basil Parmesan Tomato Sauce

3	**tablespoons olive oil**
½	**medium onion, finely minced**

- In a medium saucepan, sauté onion in oil over medium-low heat until translucent, about 10 minutes.

1	**30-ounce can stewed tomatoes, drained**
½	**teaspoon dried basil**
1	**teaspoon salt**
1	**dash black pepper**

- Add stewed tomatoes, basil, salt and black pepper. Stir. Simmer, uncovered, over low heat for 45 minutes.

1	**6-ounce can tomato paste**
2	**teaspoons sugar**
⅓	**cup freshly grated Parmesan cheese**

- Add tomato paste and mix well. Remove from heat. Add sugar and Parmesan cheese, and stir.

makes 2½ cups

Steamed Botana

When setting a buffet table, I often replace bowls of fried tortilla chips with these delicately textured, thick and spicy strips of steamed tortillas, along with plenty of sour cream, guacamole and salsa. Our guests always devour them quickly!

- 2 **teaspoons butter, softened**
- 8 **5" Steamed Tortillas** *(recipe page 62)*, **warmed**
- **salt** *(to taste)*
- **cayenne pepper** *(to taste)*

• Butter one side of each tortilla. Lightly sprinkle the buttered side with a small amount of salt and cayenne pepper. *(Remember, cayenne pepper is quite hot!)* Cut each tortilla into 5 one-inch strips.

- 3⁄4 **cup sour cream**
- 3⁄4 **cup Guacamole** *(recipe page 93)*
- 3⁄4 **cup salsa** *(your favorite)*

• Serve the tortilla strips with small bowls of sour cream, Guacamole and your favorite salsa.

makes 40

Tomato & Chive Tortilla Appetizers

Crisp and cheesy tortilla shells are filled with a delectable sour cream dip, then topped with Parmesan cheese and black olives. Always a hit with guests, this is one of my most successful appetizers.

1	**cup sour cream**
10	**fresh chives, finely minced**
1/4	**teaspoon garlic salt**
1/3	**teaspoon minced dried onion**
1	**dash Worcestershire sauce**
1	**dash black pepper**
1	**dash cayenne pepper**
1/2	**medium tomato, diced**

- In a small bowl, combine sour cream and spices. Mix well. Add diced tomato and stir gently. Cover and refrigerate until ready to serve.

36	**Cheddar Cheese Patty Shells** *(recipe page 73)*
1/3	**cup freshly grated Parmesan cheese**
18	**pitted black olives, halved**

- Fill patty shells with approximately 1½ teaspoons filling. Sprinkle each with a small amount of Parmesan cheese. Decorate each with a half of black olive.

makes 36

Tortilla Snowflakes

As a child I remember spending hours making little paper snowflakes to hang in our living room window. Now, as an adult, I spend time with my children making more snowflakes, only these are deep-fried and dusted with sugar and cinnamon. For the adult version, I sprinkle them with cayenne pepper and garlic salt, and bake in the oven until crisp.

8 **Orange Tortillas with Montmorency Cherries** *(recipe page 48)*, **or Applesauce Tortillas** *(recipe page 30)*, **or Traditional Flour Tortillas** *(recipe page 64)*

- Fold each tortilla in half, then fold in half again. Using kitchen scissors, cut out triangles along the folds. Unfold.

vegetable oil *(as needed)*

- Place vegetable oil, 1" deep, in a tall 10" skillet. Preheat oil over medium heat until hot but not smoking, about 375°.
- Deep-fry the cut tortillas on each side until golden brown, turning only once. Drain on paper towels.
- Cool completely and store in a sealed container until ready for use.

powdered sugar *(as needed)*
cinnamon sugar *(as needed)*

- Just prior to serving, lightly dust 4 snowflakes with powdered sugar. Sprinkle cinnamon sugar over the remaining 4 snowflakes.

makes 8

Southwestern Onion Soup with Tortillas & Cheese

Similar to French onion soup, but with a Southwestern flair, I make this soup only in the summer when Vidalia or Walla Walla sweet onions are in season. Other varieties of onion are much too pungent.

1	**tablespoon butter**
2	**large sweet onions, thinly sliced**
1	**teaspoon sugar**

- Melt butter in a large soup pan over low heat. Add sliced onions. Sauté until tender, about 20 to 25 minutes. Add sugar. Sauté another 5 minutes.

3	**cups Rich & Spicy Beef Stock** *(recipe page 163)*
½	**teaspoon salt**
2	**dashes black pepper**

- Add Rich & Spicy Beef Stock to onions. Season with salt and black pepper. Simmer 30 minutes.

4	**5" Risen (Yeast) Tortillas** *(recipe page 54),* **or Yogurt Tortillas** *(recipe page 66),* **or Beer Tortillas** *(recipe page 32)*
1	**cup grated Jarlsberg cheese**
1	**jalapeño chile pepper, seeds and membrane removed, thinly sliced**

- Preheat oven to broil.
- Cut each tortilla into 8 triangles.
- Ladle hot soup into 4 oven-proof soup bowls. Reconstruct 1 tortilla on top of each bowl of soup. Sprinkle each reconstructed tortilla with ¼ cup grated cheese.
- Place soup bowls on a baking sheet for ease of handling. Place baking sheet on the top rack of the oven and broil until cheese is bubbly and slightly browned, about 2 to 3 minutes. Garnish with several jalapeño chile pepper slices.

serves 4

Corn Chowder with Tortilla Crackers

Quick and easy to prepare, this thick and creamy corn chowder is sure to warm you up on a cold winter's night ..... and the light, crisp Tortilla Crackers are the perfect complement. Preparing the dough is a fun activity to share with your children.

Corn Chowder

1	**tablespoon butter**
1/4	**cup finely minced onion**
1	**stalk celery, finely minced**

- Melt butter in a medium soup pan over low heat. Add onion and celery. Sauté until tender, about 10 minutes. Remove from pan.

3	**tablespoons butter**
3	**tablespoons white flour**
1	**cup milk**
1 1/2	**cups half & half**

- In the same pan, melt butter over medium heat. Add flour. Cook and stir 1 minute. Add milk and half & half. Cook and stir until thickened and bubbly, about 10 minutes. Remove from heat.

2	**ears of corn, cooked and kernels removed**
1	**medium potato, cooked and cubed**
2	**teaspoons dried chervil**
1	**dash dried thyme**
1	**dash cayenne pepper**
1	**dash garlic powder**

- To the cream sauce, add onion mixture, corn, potato, chervil, thyme, cayenne pepper and garlic powder. Simmer over very low heat for 20 minutes.

	salt and black pepper *(to taste)*
1/8	**cup finely minced fresh chives**
	Tortilla Crackers *(recipe page 85)*

(continued on next page)

- Season with salt and black pepper. Place chowder in individual soup bowls. Garnish with fresh chives and serve with a basket of Tortilla Crackers.

serves 4

Tortilla Crackers

1¼	**cups white flour**
½	**teaspoon salt**
1	**tablespoon baking powder**
1	**dash cayenne pepper**

- Sift the dry ingredients into a medium bowl.

2	**tablespoons butter, softened**

- Cut the butter into the flour until the mixture resembles coarse meal.

3	**ounces milk**
	garlic salt *(as needed)*

- Add the milk to the flour mixture, all at once. Mix well. Gather the dough into a ball and knead briefly until the ingredients are well combined. The dough should be soft but not sticky. Divide the dough into 4 equal pieces. In the palm of your hand, roll each piece into a ball, then flatten slightly. Place the rounds of dough on one half of a dish towel and cover them with the other half. Let rest 15 minutes.

- Preheat oven to 400°.

- On a lightly floured board, roll out 1 piece of dough into an 8" circle. Using a pasta cutter *(or knife)* cut the tortilla into 8 triangles. Place triangles on an ungreased baking sheet, making sure the edges do not touch. Roll and cut the remaining 3 pieces of dough and place on baking sheet. Sprinkle each piece lightly with garlic salt.

- Bake for 8 to 10 minutes, or until crisp and golden brown. Cool on a rack, lined with paper towels. Store in an airtight container.

makes 32 crackers

Creamy Mushroom Soup with Floating Tortillas

This exquisite soup is made with a rich vegetable broth and whole button mushrooms. For the crowning touch, I like to provide a garnish of fresh lavender.

3	**cups water**
1	**pound small whole button mushrooms, stems removed and reserved**
1	**stalk celery, finely sliced**
1	**carrot** *(with peel),* **finely chopped**
2	**scallions, thinly sliced**
½	**teaspoon fresh thyme**
2	**dashes black pepper**

- Heat water in a medium saucepan to boiling.
- Add mushroom stems, celery, carrot, scallions, thyme and black pepper. Simmer, uncovered, until liquid is reduced to ½ cup, about 1 hour.
- Strain, reserving broth. Discard vegetables.

4	**tablespoons butter**
⅓	**cup white flour**
5	**cups milk**
2	**cups half & half**
1	**teaspoon salt**
2	**ounces cream cheese, softened**
2	**tablespoons thinly sliced scallions**

- Melt butter in a large soup pan over medium-low heat. Add flour. Cook and stir 1 minute.
- Add vegetable broth, milk, half & half and salt. Cook and stir until thickened and bubbly, about 10 minutes. Reduce the heat to low.

(continued on next page)

- Add cream cheese, scallions and mushroom caps. Mix well. Simmer, uncovered, until mushrooms are tender, about 30 minutes.

prepare half the dough for Lavender Tortillas with Garlic Chives *(recipe page 45),* **or Cottage Cheese Tortillas** *(recipe page 42),* **or "Corn" Tortillas with Caramelized Onion** *(recipe page 40)*

6 sprigs fresh lavender

- To make 1" tortillas, divide dough into 36 balls. Finish making the tortillas by following the directions located on page 10 *(About Making Tortillas)*. Begin with step number 6.
- Serve soup in individual bowls with several miniature tortillas floating on top. Serve the remaining tortillas on the side. Garnish each with a sprig of fresh lavender.

serves 6

Tortilla Soup (with Fried Tortilla Balls)

The fried tortilla balls in this soup remain crisp at first, then slowly soak up the rich chicken broth. Remember that a good homemade broth takes about five hours to prepare, so I usually make it a day ahead of time.

prepare half the dough for Cheddar Cheese Tortillas *(recipe page 39),* **or Jalapeño Tortillas** *(recipe page 44),* **or Traditional Flour Tortillas** *(recipe page 64)*

- Preheat oven to 200°.
- Divide the dough into 20 pieces. Form each piece into a ball and flatten slightly.

vegetable oil *(as needed)*

- In an 8" skillet, preheat ½" of vegetable oil over medium-high heat until hot but not smoking.
- In hot oil, deep-fry the tortilla balls, 10 at a time, until crisp and golden brown, about 1 minute per side. Drain on a paper towel and place in the oven to keep warm. Continue with the remaining 10 pieces of dough.

4 cups Strong Brown Chicken Stock *(recipe page 162),* **hot**
1 tablespoon minced fresh parsley

- Place hot Strong Brown Chicken Stock in 4 individual soup bowls. Top each bowl of soup with 3 to 5 tortilla balls and a pinch of fresh parsley.

serves 4

Chicken Apple Tortilla Salad

Mounded on a tasty Applesauce Tortilla, this chicken apple salad can first be eaten with a fork, then rolled up and eaten like a burrito. It's delicious and easy to prepare.

1 **cup sour cream**
1 **tablespoon mayonnaise**
1/4 **cup milk**

- In a medium bowl, combine sour cream, mayonnaise and milk.

1 **cup finely diced apples, peeled**
1 **stalk celery, thinly sliced**
1/3 **cup slivered almonds, toasted**
1/2 **teaspoon minced dried onion**
1 **cup medium diced cooked chicken, skin removed**
1 1/2 **cups cooked macaroni, cooled**
salt and black pepper *(to taste)*

- Add apples, celery, almonds and onion to sour cream mixture. Stir. Add chicken and macaroni. Mix well. Season with salt and black pepper. Refrigerate until ready to serve.

4 **whole leaves of leaf lettuce, washed and dried**
4 **Applesauce Tortillas** *(recipe page 30),* **warmed, or Parmesan Cheese Tortillas** *(recipe page 49),* **or Bran Tortillas** *(recipe page 34)*
1/2 **cup finely grated Cheddar cheese**
1/2 **cup Homemade Croutons** *(recipe page 97)*
1/4 **cup raisins**

- Put a lettuce leaf on top of each tortilla. Place a mound of chicken apple salad on top of the lettuce. Sprinkle each with a little cheese, a few Homemade Croutons and raisins.

serves 4

Chilled Asparagus on a Tortilla with Savory Raspberry Sauce

A light summertime meal with an addicting red raspberry sauce, this salad is best served over a fresh Butter Tortilla. It adds a richness in texture without detracting from the salad's delicate flavors.

Chilled Asparagus on a Tortilla

1 bunch fresh asparagus, trimmed to 6" long spears

- Steam asparagus until tender, about 10 to 12 minutes. Drain well and cool. Cover and refrigerate for at least 1 hour.

4 Butter Tortillas *(recipe page 35),* **warmed, or Cottage Cheese Tortillas** *(recipe page 42),* **or Sour Cream & Potato Tortillas** *(recipe page 59)*
8 whole leaves romaine lettuce, washed and dried
½ cup Savory Raspberry Sauce *(recipe page 91)*
¼ cup coarsely chopped walnuts
12 fresh *(or thawed)* **red raspberries**

- Place 1 tortilla on each salad plate. Top each tortilla with 2 whole romaine lettuce leaves and ¼ of the chilled asparagus.
- Remove Savory Raspberry Sauce from refrigerator. Using a whisk, blend well. Drizzle 2 tablespoons of sauce over the asparagus on each salad. Garnish with chopped walnuts and a few fresh raspberries.

serves 4

Savory Raspberry Sauce

1½ tablespoons butter
¼ cup minced purple shallots

• Melt butter in a medium saucepan over low heat. Add minced shallots. Sauté until tender, about 2 to 3 minutes.

2 cups fresh *(or frozen)* **red raspberries**
½ cup brut Champagne
2 cups Strong Brown Chicken Stock *(recipe page 162)*
3 teaspoons minced fresh basil
1 dash dry hot mustard
1 dash white pepper

• Add raspberries, Champagne, Strong Brown Chicken Stock, basil, dry hot mustard and white pepper. Simmer over very low heat for 30 minutes. Remove from heat.

• Using a large, finely meshed strainer, strain juice into a small saucepan. Discard raspberry pulp.

3½ tablespoons sugar
1 tablespoon butter
1 dash salt *(or to taste)*

• Add sugar to strained juice. Simmer over medium-low heat until sauce is reduced to ½ cup, about 30 minutes. Remove from heat. Add butter and salt. Stir well. Cover and refrigerate at least 1 hour. Blend well, with a whisk, before using.

makes ½ cup

Cucumber Tortilla Salad with Parmesan Tomatoes

A crisp, cool cucumber salad over warm, cheese-broiled tomato slices, supported by a fresh tortilla, makes a quick and easy summertime lunch.

1	**cup sour cream**
¼	**cup half & half**
¼	**cup finely sliced scallions**
½	**teaspoon ground sumac**
	salt and black pepper *(to taste)*

- In a small bowl, make dressing by combining sour cream, half & half, scallions, sumac, salt and black pepper. Cover and chill 1 hour.

3	**cucumbers, seeds removed, and coarsely diced**
¾	**cup whole cashews**
1	**cup Homemade Croutons** *(recipe page 97)*
	salt and black pepper *(to taste)*

- In a large bowl, combine diced cucumber, cashews and Homemade Croutons. Add the chilled dressing. Mix well. Season with salt and black pepper.

12	**large slices tomato, ¼" thick**
½	**cup freshly grated Parmesan cheese**
6	**Red Bell Pepper Tortillas** *(recipe page 52),* **warmed, or Black Olive & Sour Cream Tortillas** *(recipe page 33),* **or Bran Tortillas** *(recipe page 34)*

Preheat oven to broil.

Place the tomato slices on a large baking sheet. Sprinkle about 1 teaspoon Parmesan cheese over each. Broil 2 to 3 minutes, or until cheese is bubbly and slightly browned.

Arrange 2 broiled tomato slices in the center of each tortilla. Top with a generous amount of cucumber salad and a sprinkle of Parmesan cheese.

serves 6

Guacamole

This spicy avocado dip is accented with ripe plum tomatoes, green scallions and ground jalapeño chile pepper.

- 2 **medium avocados, peeled and pit removed**
- ½ **teaspoon fresh lime juice**

• Place avocado and lime juice in a small bowl. Using a fork, mash the avocado until smooth.

- ½ **cup diced plum tomato**
- 1 **scallion, thinly sliced**
- 1 **tablespoon sour cream**
- ¼ **teaspoon ground jalapeño chile pepper** *(or 1 teaspoon fresh minced)*
- 2 **dashes garlic powder**
- **salt and black pepper** *(to taste)*

• Add tomato, scallion, sour cream, ground jalapeño chile pepper and garlic powder to the avocado mixture. Stir until well combined. Season with salt and black pepper. Stir well.

• Place Guacamole in a two-cup plastic container. Place plastic wrap directly on the Guacamole and smooth with fingertips to remove air pockets. *(Avocados discolor when they're exposed to oxygen. The plastic wrap will help slow down this process.)* Seal with a plastic lid and refrigerate until chilled, about 30 minutes.

makes approximately 1¼ cups

Taco Salad

A great summertime meal, this taco salad is a good way to use up small amounts of leftover chicken or beef. For a special treat, I serve it with cactus salsa, instead of the traditional tomato salsa.

1⅓	**cups Spicy Frijoles** *(recipe page 101)*, **warmed**
4	**"Corn" Tortillas with Caramelized Onion** *(recipe page 40)*, **warmed, or Cream Cheese Tortillas** *(recipe page 43)*, **or Sun-Dried Tomato Tortillas** *(recipe page 61)*

- Spread ⅓ cup Spicy Frijoles over each tortilla.

2	**cups shredded iceberg lettuce**
1	**cup shredded cooked chicken** *(or beef)*, **skin removed**
1	**medium tomato, finely diced**
1	**cup finely diced Monterey Jack cheese**
½	**cup sliced black olives**
1	**avocado, peeled and pit removed, thinly sliced**
	sour cream *(as needed)*
	salsa *(your favorite)*

- Top each tortilla with ½ cup lettuce. Place ¼ of the chicken, tomatoes, cheese, black olives and avocado on top.
- Garnish with a dollop of sour cream and serve with plenty of salsa.

serves 4

Tortilla Salad with Buttermilk Caesar Dressing & Homemade Croutons

My father first introduced me to the delicious complexities of caesar salad as a child, and I have loved sampling variations ever since. This recipe is enhanced with a creamy buttermilk dressing and crunchy, easy-to-make garlic croutons.

Tortilla Salad

1 **large head romaine lettuce, separated, washed and dried**
1 **thin slice red cabbage, separated**
½ **cup Buttermilk Caesar Dressing** *(recipe page 96)*
1¼ **cups freshly grated Parmesan cheese**
2 **cups Homemade Croutons** *(recipe page 97)*

• Tear lettuce into large bite-size pieces. Place in a large salad bowl. Add sliced cabbage. Add Buttermilk Caesar Dressing and toss until lettuce and cabbage are well coated. Lightly toss in Parmesan cheese and Homemade Croutons.

6 **Parmesan Cheese Tortillas** *(recipe page 49)*, **warmed, or Buttermilk Tortillas** *(recipe page 36)*, **or Lemon Spinach Tortillas** *(recipe page 46)*
12 **large pitted black olives**
black pepper *(to taste)*

• Place tortillas on individual salad plates. Top with a generous portion of salad and garnish with olives and freshly ground black pepper.

serves 6

Buttermilk Caesar Dressing

1/3	**cup fresh buttermilk**
2	**tablespoons olive oil**
2	**tablespoons fresh lemon juice**
2	**teaspoons Dijon mustard**
1	**teaspoon anchovy paste**
1	**teaspoon Worcestershire sauce**
1	**dash Tabasco sauce**
1/8	**teaspoon black pepper**
	paste from 1 head of Vermouth Roasted Garlic *(recipe page 160)*

- Combine buttermilk, olive oil, lemon juice, mustard, anchovy paste, Worcestershire sauce, Tabasco sauce and black pepper. Mix well.
- Add garlic paste. Mix well again.
- Refrigerate in an airtight container until ready for use.

makes approximately ½ cup

Homemade Croutons

- **2½ tablespoons butter**
- **1 clove garlic, pressed**
- **1 small purple shallot, pressed**
- **1 dash salt**
- **2 cups bread cubes, ¼" thick by ½" wide**

- Preheat oven to 400°.
- Melt butter in the bottom of a 13" x 9" baking dish in the oven, about 2 minutes. Add garlic, shallot and salt. Mix well.
- Add bread cubes and toss until evenly coated. Bake, stirring every 10 minutes, until light brown and crisp, about 20 to 30 minutes.
- Cool to room temperature. Place in an airtight container until ready for use.

makes 2 cups

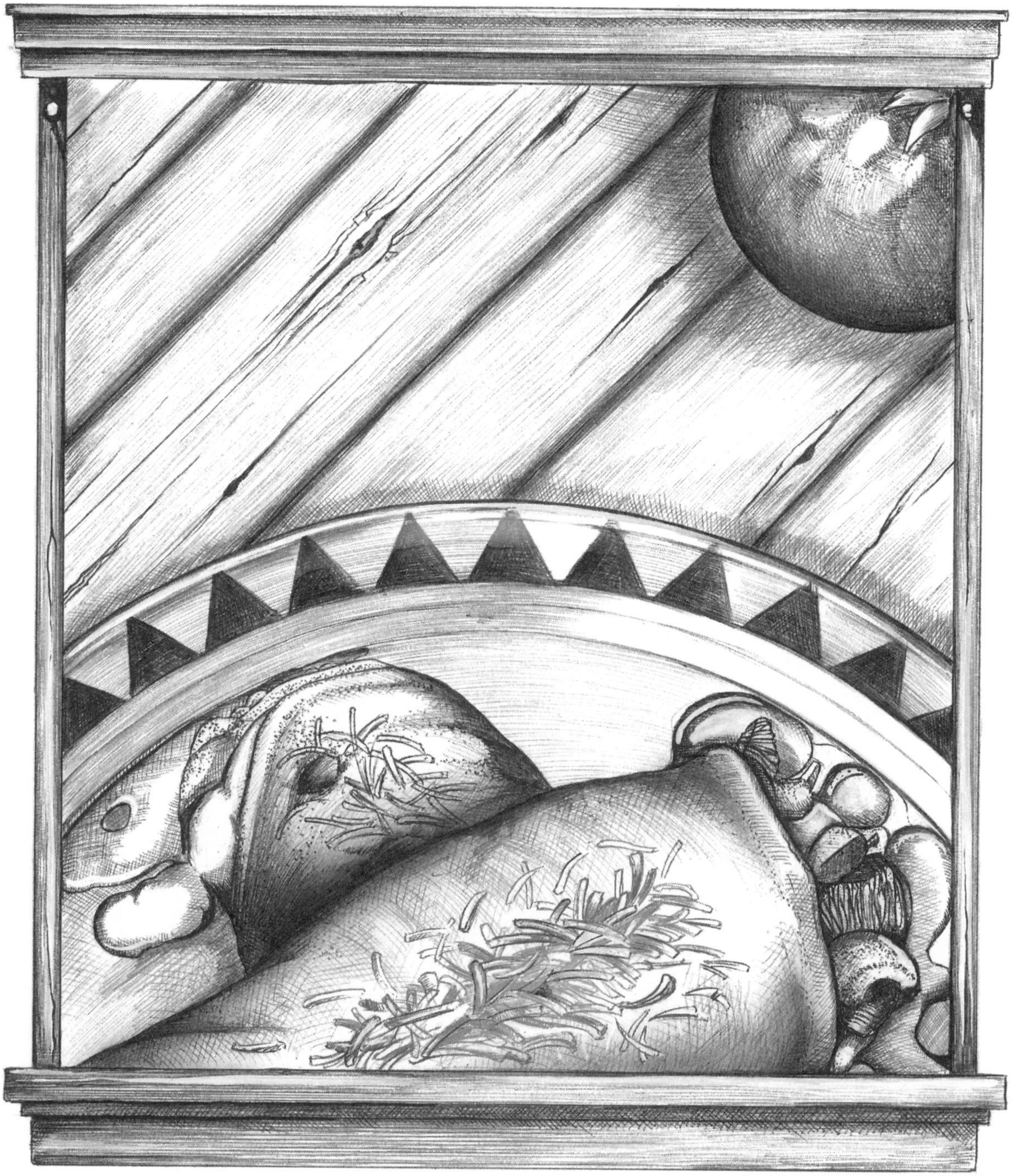

Burritos & Enchiladas

Cheese Burritos with Spicy Frijoles

A fresh, thick and chewy tortilla transforms this traditional burrito into something really special. You can make these in advance by omitting the tomatoes and avocado slices, and then freezing them.

Cheese Burritos

- 3 **cups Spicy Frijoles** *(recipe page 101),* **hot**
- 8 **Risen (Yeast) Tortillas** *(recipe page 54),* **warmed, or Cheddar Cheese Tortillas** *(recipe page 39),* **or Sour Cream & Potato Tortillas** *(recipe page 59)*
- 1½ **cups grated Cheddar cheese** *(or Monterey Jack)*
- 1 **large tomato, finely diced**
- 1 **avocado, peeled and pit removed, thinly sliced**
- **sour cream** *(as needed)*
- **salsa** *(your favorite)*
- 1 **jalapeño chile pepper, seeds and membrane removed, thinly sliced**

- Spread a small amount of Spicy Frijoles on one side of each tortilla. Top with cheese, tomato and avocado slices
- Roll up and serve with sour cream and your favorite salsa.
- Garnish with jalapeño chile pepper slices.

serves 4 to 6

Spicy Frijoles

- **1 30-ounce can refried beans**
- **3 scallions, thinly sliced**
- **1 teaspoon ground cumin**
- **½ teaspoon dried minced jalapeño chile pepper** *(or 1 teaspoon fresh minced)*
- **¼ teaspoon ground coriander**
- **¼ teaspoon garlic powder**
- **¼ teaspoon ground black pepper**

• Place refried beans, scallions and spices in a medium saucepan. Simmer, uncovered, over low heat for 45 minutes, stirring often.

makes 3 cups

Kiwi Chicken Burritos

This Hawaiian-style chicken burrito is prepared with macadamia nuts, fresh kiwi and wildflower honey. The chicken breasts need to marinate for about three hours, so begin this recipe early in the day.

- 5 **tablespoons olive oil**
- 3 **tablespoons fresh lime juice**
- 3 **tablespoons finely minced fresh chives**
- 2 **tablespoons minced fresh lemon balm** *(or 1 dash fresh lemon juice)*
- 1 **kiwi, peeled and thinly sliced**
- ¼ **teaspoon black pepper**
- 2 **boneless chicken breasts, skin removed**

• In a shallow, glass dish *(with lid)*, combine olive oil, lime juice, chives, lemon balm, kiwi and black pepper. Stir.

• Place chicken breasts in marinade and coat well. Cover and refrigerate for 3 hours.

- ⅓ **cup white flour**
- ⅛ **teaspoon paprika**
- 1 **dash cayenne pepper**
- 1 **dash salt**

• In a medium bowl, combine flour, paprika, cayenne and salt. Mix well.

• Slice the marinated chicken into ½" wide strips.

• Dredge chicken through the flour mixture until evenly coated.

- 2 **tablespoons olive oil**
- 2 **tablespoons wildflower honey**
- ⅓ **cup whole macadamia nuts**
- 2 **tablespoons finely minced fresh chives**

• Preheat a 10" skillet over medium-high heat.

(continued on next page)

- Coat the skillet evenly with olive oil. Add coated chicken. Stir-fry until golden brown, about 10 minutes.
- Add honey and continue cooking, about 2 to 3 minutes. Add macadamia nuts and chives. Stir.

8 **Buttermilk Tortillas** *(recipe page 36),* **warmed, or Jalapeño Tortillas** *(recipe page 44),* **or Yogurt Soda Tortillas** *(recipe page 67)*

sour cream *(as needed)*

1 **kiwi, peeled and sliced**

- Place chicken on one side of each tortilla. Top with a dollop of sour cream and fresh kiwi slices. Fold the other side of the tortilla over the filling before serving.

serves 4 to 6

Breakfast Burrito

The taste of this excellent homemade breakfast burrito bears little resemblance to its popular cousin sold in fast food restaurants.

12 skinless pork sausage links

- Cook sausage in a large skillet over medium heat until well browned and thoroughly cooked. Drain on paper towels.

6 eggs
2 tablespoons sour cream
2 tablespoons milk
1/8 teaspoon salt
1 dash black pepper

- Break eggs into a medium bowl and whisk until fluffy. Add sour cream, milk, salt and black pepper. Mix well.

1 tablespoon butter

- Melt butter in a large skillet over medium heat. Add egg mixture. Cook and stir until cooked and firm.

6 Bran Tortillas *(recipe page 34)*, **warmed, or Buttermilk & Potato Tortillas** *(recipe page 37)*, **or Oatmeal Tortillas** *(recipe page 47)*
pure maple syrup *(as needed)*, **heated**

- Place 2 sausage links on each of the 6 tortillas. Top each tortilla with 1/6 of the egg mixture. Roll up the tortillas and serve with pure maple syrup.

serves 4 to 6

Marinated Beef Burritos

Sautéed mushrooms and flavorful marinated beef make delicious burritos when wrapped in fresh tortillas. You can make the beef marinade in advance and then refrigerate it until needed, minimizing last minute preparations.

1	**pound top sirloin, thinly sliced**
½	**cup soy sauce**
¼	**cup rice wine**
¼	**cup water**
¼	**teaspoon ground ginger**
1	**teaspoon dry mustard**
1	**clove garlic, finely minced**
2	**tablespoons minced onion**

- In a medium bowl, combine beef, soy sauce, rice wine, water and spices. Cover and refrigerate for 1 hour.

1	**teaspoon vegetable oil**
2	**cups sliced mushrooms**
5	**scallions, thinly sliced**

- Heat oil in a large skillet over medium heat. Add mushrooms and scallions. Sauté until tender, about 10 minutes.
- Drain beef mixture, discarding the liquid. Add marinated beef to the sautéed mushrooms. Stir-fry until tender, about 4 minutes. Remove from heat.

4	**Cottage Cheese Tortillas** *(recipe page 42),* **warmed, or Scallion Tortillas** *(recipe page 57),* **or Sourdough Tortillas** *(recipe page 60)*
	hot Chinese mustard *(as needed)*

- Place a generous amount of beef mixture on one side of each tortilla and roll up. Serve with a small bowl of hot Chinese mustard on the side.

serves 2 to 4

Anaheim Beef Enchiladas

These beef enchiladas are made with sautéed anaheim chile pepper, then topped with a spicy brown sauce, sliced Provolone cheese and toasted almonds. Because of its beautiful presentation, this is a great dish to serve for company.

1½ tablespoons butter
½ cup minced yellow onion
½ stalk celery, finely minced
1 anaheim chile pepper, seeds and membrane removed, finely minced
½ cup seedless raisins

• Melt butter in a large skillet over medium-low heat. Add onion, celery and minced anaheim chile pepper. Sauté until tender, about 15 minutes. Remove from heat. Add raisins. Cover and let sit 10 minutes.

1½ cups cooked and shredded beef
¾ cup diced fresh tomato, seeds removed
2 tablespoons minced fresh parsley
2 dashes salt *(or to taste)*
⅛ teaspoon black pepper *(or to taste)*

• In a medium bowl combine beef, tomato, parsley, salt and black pepper. Add the sautéed vegetables and mix well. Refrigerate until ready for use.

2½ tablespoons butter
3 tablespoons white flour
2 cups Strong Brown Chicken Stock *(recipe page 162)*
1 dash salt
1 dash black pepper

• Melt butter in a small saucepan over medium-low heat. Add flour and cook 1 minute, stirring constantly. Add Strong Brown Chicken Stock. Cook and stir until thickened and bubbly, about 10 minutes. Season with salt and black pepper.

(continued on next page)

- Place ⅓ of the brown sauce, evenly, in the bottom of a 13" x 9" baking dish.
- Preheat oven to 375°.

8 **Beer Tortillas** *(recipe page 32),* **or Sour Cream Tortillas** *(recipe page 58),* **or Lavender Tortillas with Garlic Chives** *(recipe page 45)*

- Place ½ cup of the filling on one side of a tortilla. Starting on the filled side, roll up the tortilla and place in the prepared baking dish, seam side down. Continue with the remaining 7 tortillas.

½ **pound sliced Provolone cheese**
¼ **cup coarsely chopped almonds, toasted**
1 **tablespoon minced fresh parsley**

- Pour remaining brown sauce over tortillas and top with sliced cheese. Sprinkle almonds and parsley on top.
- Bake for 25 to 30 minutes, or until lightly browned and bubbly.

serves 4 to 6

Cheese Enchiladas

These delicious rich and creamy cheese enchiladas are made with a mixture of white Cheddar cheese, cream cheese and fresh green chives.

2½ tablespoons butter
3 tablespoons white flour
1½ cups Strong Brown Chicken Stock *(recipe page 162)*
1 cup milk
1 dash salt
1 dash black pepper

- Melt butter in a medium saucepan over medium-low heat. Add flour. Cook and stir 1 minute. Add Strong Brown Chicken Stock, milk, salt and black pepper. Cook and stir until thickened and bubbly, about 10 minutes. Remove from heat. Pour ¾ cup chicken sauce evenly into a 13" x 9" baking dish.

12 ounces cream cheese, softened
¼ cup minced fresh chives
¼ teaspoon black pepper
3¾ cups grated white Cheddar cheese

- In a medium bowl, combine cream cheese, chives and black pepper. Mix well. Add 3 cups of the grated Cheddar cheese *(reserve the rest)*. Mix thoroughly.

8 Sun-Dried Tomato Tortillas *(recipe page 61),* **or Jalapeño Tortillas** *(recipe page 44),* **or Lavender Tortillas with Garlic Chives** *(recipe page 45)*

- Preheat oven to 375°.

- Place approximately ⅓ cup of the cheese mixture on one side of each tortilla. Starting on the filled side, roll up each tortilla. Place filled tortillas in baking dish, seam side down. Pour remaining chicken sauce over tortillas. Sprinkle the rest of the Cheddar cheese on top.

- Bake for 25 to 30 minutes, or until bubbly and lightly browned.

serves 4 to 6

Chicken Enchiladas

An exceptionally delicious enchilada dish that everyone loves, the secret to the good flavor lies in the rich brown chicken stock.

- **3** **cups cooked and shredded chicken, skin removed**
- **4** **scallions, thinly sliced**
- **3** **plum tomatoes, seeds removed, and coarsely diced**
- **1** **cup grated Jarlsberg cheese**
- **salt and black pepper** *(to taste)*

• In a medium bowl, combine chicken, scallions, tomatoes *(reserve 3 tablespoons)* and cheese. Season with salt and black pepper. Refrigerate until ready for use.

- **2½** **tablespoons butter**
- **3** **tablespoons white flour**
- **2** **cups Strong Brown Chicken Stock** *(recipe page 162)*
- **⅛** **teaspoon black pepper**

• Melt butter in a medium saucepan over medium heat. Add flour. Cook and stir 1 minute. Add Strong Brown Chicken Stock and black pepper. Continue to cook and stir until thickened and bubbly, about 10 minutes. Remove from heat. Pour ⅓ of the sauce in the bottom of a 13" x 9" baking dish.

- **8** **Black Olive & Sour Cream Tortillas** *(recipe page 33),* **or Red Bell Pepper Tortillas** *(recipe page 52),* **or Potato & Yogurt Tortillas** *(recipe page 51)*
- **½** **cup grated Jarlsberg cheese**
- **2** **tablespoons thinly sliced scallions**

• Preheat oven to 375°.

• Place ½ cup chicken mixture on one side of a tortilla. Roll it up and place in the baking dish, seam side down. Continue with the remaining 7 tortillas. Pour the remaining sauce over the filled tortillas. Sprinkle grated cheese, scallions and reserved diced tomato over top. Bake for 20 to 25 minutes, or until lightly browned and bubbly.

serves 4 to 6

Chicken & Pistachio Enchiladas

These chicken and cheese filled enchiladas are baked in a savory sauce, then topped with sour cream and roasted pistachios. It makes a wonderful meal when served with a light salad and thick, crusty slices of bread.

- **1** **teaspoon butter**
- **¾** **cup minced fresh mushrooms**
- **2** **cups cooked and shredded chicken, skin removed**
- **1** **cup grated Fontina cheese**
- **¼** **cup finely sliced scallions**
- **¼** **teaspoon fresh minced thyme**

• Melt butter in a medium saucepan over medium-high heat. Add mushrooms and sauté until tender, about 5 minutes. Cool to room temperature. Add chicken, cheese, scallions and thyme. Mix well. Cover and chill for 30 minutes.

- **3** **tablespoons butter**
- **3½** **tablespoons white flour**
- **2** **cups Strong Brown Chicken Stock** *(recipe page 162)*
- **1** **dash salt**
- **1** **dash freshly ground green peppercorns**

• Melt butter in a small saucepan over medium heat. Add flour. Cook and stir 1 minute. Add Strong Brown Chicken Stock, salt and pepper. Cook and stir until thickened and bubbly, about 10 minutes. Remove from heat.

- **8** **Buttermilk Tortillas** *(recipe page 36),* **or Whole Wheat Tortillas** *(recipe page 65),* **or Orange Tortillas with Montmorency Cherries** *(recipe page 48)*
- **1** **cup grated sharp Cheddar cheese**
- **¾** **cup sour cream**
- **½** **cup shelled pistachios, roasted**

• Preheat oven to 375°.

(continued on next page)

- Place ⅓ of the sauce in a 13" x 9" baking dish.
- Place ⅛ of the chicken mixture on one side of a tortilla. Roll up the tortilla and place in baking dish, seam side down. Continue with the remaining 7 tortillas.
- Pour the remaining sauce over filled tortillas. Sprinkle the top with grated Cheddar cheese.
- Bake for 25 to 30 minutes, or until golden brown and bubbly.
- Serve on individual plates. Garnish with a dollop of sour cream and several roasted pistachios.

serves 4 to 6

Chicken & Zucchini Enchiladas

This is a great dish to make during the summer when overzealous home gardeners give away huge sacks of zucchini to neighbors and friends.

1 teaspoon butter
1 small zucchini, peeled and cut into ¼" cubes
5 medium mushrooms, finely chopped

- Melt butter in a large skillet over medium heat. Sauté zucchini and mushrooms until tender, about 10 minutes. Cool to room temperature.

2 cups cooked and shredded chicken, skin removed
½ cup thinly sliced black olives
1½ cups grated Provolone cheese

- Add chicken, black olives and cheese to sautéed mushroom mixture. Mix well.

10 Sun-Dried Tomato Tortillas *(recipe page 61),* **or Yogurt Tortillas** *(recipe page 66),* **or Romano Cheese & Chive Tortillas** *(recipe page 56)*
2 cups Brown Sauce II *(recipe page 166)*
⅓ cup freshly grated Parmesan cheese

- Preheat oven to 375°.
- Place ½ cup of Brown Sauce II, evenly, in the bottom of a 13" x 9" baking dish.
- Place ½ cup of the chicken mixture on one side of a tortilla. Starting on the filled side, roll up the tortilla. Place it in the baking dish, seam side down. Continue with the remaining 9 tortillas. Pour the remaining Brown Sauce II over the filled tortillas. Top with freshly grated Parmesan cheese.
- Bake for 30 to 35 minutes, or until bubbly and lightly browned.

serves 6

Shredded Beef & Eggplant Enchiladas

The flavors in this dish are so subtle and well blended, that even people who are not eggplant lovers will enjoy it. Serve it with sour cream and fresh salsa on the side.

1 tablespoon butter
½ small onion, finely chopped
2 cups thinly sliced mushrooms
1½ cups small cubes eggplant, peeled

• Melt butter in a large skillet over medium-low heat. Add onions and sauté until translucent, about 10 minutes. Add mushrooms and eggplant. Sauté until tender, about 15 minutes. Remove from heat and drain.

1 pound chuck steak, cooked and shredded
1½ cups grated Monterey Jack cheese
1 teaspoon dried parsley *(or 2 tablespoons fresh minced)*
½ teaspoon dried minced green bell pepper *(or 2 tablespoons fresh minced)*
salt and black pepper *(to taste)*

• In a large bowl, combine sautéed mushrooms and eggplant, beef, cheese, parsley and bell pepper. Mix well. Season with salt and black pepper.

10 Jalapeño Tortillas *(recipe page 44)***, or Black Olive & Sour Cream Tortillas** *(recipe page 33)***, or Butter Tortillas** *(recipe page 35)*

• Preheat oven to 375°.

2 cups Brown Sauce I *(recipe page 164)*
½ cup grated Monterey Jack cheese

• Place ½ cup of Brown Sauce I, evenly, in a 13" x 9" baking dish.

• Place ½ cup of the beef and eggplant mixture on one side of a tortilla. Starting on the filled side, roll up the tortilla. Place rolled tortilla, seam side down, in the baking dish. Continue with the remaining 9 tortillas. Cover with the remaining Brown Sauce II and top with grated cheese. Bake for 30 to 35 minutes, or until bubbly and lightly browned.

serves 6

New York Steak Enchiladas with Chardonnay Mushroom Sauce

My Midwestern upbringing combined with a great fondness for rich French sauces influenced the creation of these truly gourmet enchiladas. The New York steaks are grilled until medium-rare, sliced very thin, tucked into a tortilla, then baked in my wonderful Chardonnay Mushroom Sauce (which is also good on fresh pasta).

New York Steak Enchiladas

2 8-ounce New York steaks

- Grill steaks over hot coals until medium-rare. Let cool and then slice thinly.

3/4 cup grated Provolone cheese
3/4 cup grated sharp Cheddar cheese
2 cups Chardonnay Mushroom Sauce *(recipe page 115),* **heated**

- In a medium bowl, combine sliced steak, grated cheeses and 1/3 cup of the Chardonnay Mushroom Sauce. Mix well.

10 Cream Cheese Tortillas *(recipe page 43),* **or Jalapeño Tortillas** *(recipe page 44),* **or Yogurt Tortillas** *(recipe page 66)*

- Preheat oven to 375°.
- Place 1/10 of the steak and cheese mixture on one side of a tortilla. Roll up the tortilla and place in a buttered 13" x 9" baking dish, seam side down. Continue with the remaining 9 tortillas.

1/4 cup grated Provolone cheese
1/4 cup grated Cheddar cheese

- Pour the remaining Chardonnay Mushroom Sauce over filled tortillas and sprinkle the top with grated cheeses.
- Bake for 25 to 30 minutes, or until golden brown and bubbly.

serves 6

Chardonnay Mushroom Sauce

2	**cups thinly sliced mushrooms**
¼	**cup Chardonnay** *(or dry white wine)*
1	**cup milk**

- Combine mushrooms and Chardonnay in a small saucepan. Add milk and bring to a boil over medium heat *(the milk will curdle slightly)*. Reduce the heat to low and simmer for 15 minutes. Remove from heat.

2	**tablespoons butter**
2	**tablespoons white flour**
½	**teaspoon salt**
⅛	**teaspoon white pepper**

- Melt butter in a small saucepan over medium heat. Add flour, cook and stir 1 minute. Add the mushroom mixture, salt and white pepper. Cook and stir until thickened and bubbly, about 5 minutes.

makes 2 cups

Main Dishes

French Toasted Breakfast Tortillas

On lazy weekend mornings, our whole family joins in the preparation of these breakfast tortillas for brunch. They make a great change of pace from traditional French toast, especially if you're out of bread!

3 **large eggs**
2 **tablespoons sour cream**
3 **tablespoons milk**
1 **dash salt**
1 **dash cinnamon**

- In a small bowl, beat eggs until fluffy. Add sour cream, milk, salt and cinnamon. Mix well.

dough for Applesauce Tortillas *(recipe page 30),* **or Orange Tortillas with Montmorency Cherries** *(recipe page 48),* **or Cream Cheese Tortillas** *(recipe page 43)*
2 **teaspoons butter**

- Preheat oven to 200°.
- Divide dough into 12 pieces. Let rest 15 minutes.
- On a lightly floured board, roll out 1 piece of dough into an 8" circle. Dip the tortilla into the egg mixture, making sure that both sides are evenly coated.
- Preheat a heavy skillet over medium heat.
- Melt butter in the preheated skillet. Fry the tortilla, turning only once, until golden brown, about 1½ minutes on each side. Place the cooked tortilla on an oven-proof platter and keep warm in the oven. Continue to roll and fry the remaining 11 tortillas.

sweet butter *(as needed)*
pure maple syrup *(as needed),* **warmed**

- Serve with sweet butter and pure maple syrup.

serves 4

Tortilla Eggs Benedict

This is my version of the classic eggs benedict, which has become our family tradition to serve for brunch on New Year's Day.

1 tablespoon butter
water *(as needed)*
8 eggs
1 dash salt
1 dash black pepper

- Melt butter in a 10" skillet over medium heat. Add water to ½" in depth. Cover and heat water until steamy. Crack eggs into steaming water. Poach eggs until whites are set and the yolks are soft, about 3 minutes. Season with salt and black pepper.

4 large slices grilled ham *(or 16 slices crisp bacon)*
4 Cheddar Cheese Tortillas *(recipe page 39),* **warmed, or Risen (Yeast) Tortillas** *(recipe page 54),* **or Potato Tortillas** *(recipe page 50)*
½ cup Hollandaise Sauce *(recipe page 125),* **heated**
freshly ground green peppercorns *(to taste)*
4 sprigs fresh basil

- Place 1 slice of grilled ham *(or 2 slices bacon)* in the center of each tortilla. Place 2 eggs on top. Drizzle ¼ of the Hollandaise Sauce over eggs.
- Garnish with several dashes of freshly ground green peppercorns and a sprig of fresh basil.

serves 4

Apple Raspberry Butter & Tortillas

My children love to eat this jam for breakfast with sweet butter and fresh warm tortillas. It makes a great wintertime treat.

4 cups frozen, unsweetened red raspberries *(with juice),* **thawed**
½ cup water

- Place raspberries *(with juice)* and water in a large saucepan. Cook over medium-low heat for 20 minutes. Strain juice through a wire mesh strainer. Discard pulp. Return juice to saucepan.

6 cups coarsely diced Granny Smith apples, peeled
1 cup sugar
1 dash salt

- Add diced apples, sugar and salt to the raspberry juice. Cover and cook over low heat for 20 to 30 minutes, or until apples are tender.
- Preheat oven to 325°.
- Using a potato masher *(or a fork),* mash the apples.
- Pour mixture into a deep sided 13" x 9" baking dish. Bake in the oven for 1½ to 2 hours, or until very thick, stirring every 30 minutes.
- Cool to room temperature.

1 cup frozen, unsweetened red raspberries *(without juice),* **thawed**

- Add 1 cup raspberries to cooled jam. Mix gently.
- Place jam in a sealable container and refrigerate.

(continued on next page)

8 **Oatmeal Tortillas** *(recipe page 47),* **or Traditional Flour Tortillas** *(recipe page 64),* **or Applesauce Tortillas** *(recipe page 30)*
sweet butter *(as needed)*

- Preheat oven to 300°.
- Wrap tortillas tightly in aluminum foil. Place in oven for 10 to 15 minutes, or until warm.
- Serve the Apple Raspberry Butter with tortillas and sweet butter.

serves 4

Vegetable Frittata Wrapped in Tortillas

A frittata is similar to an omelet, only I find that it is easier to make. This one is prepared with fresh mushrooms, sliced zucchini, potatoes and sun-dried tomatoes.

1½ tablespoons butter
6 sun-dried tomatoes *(not packed in oil),* **chopped small**

• Heat butter in a small saucepan until hot. Remove from heat and add sun-dried tomatoes. Let sit 15 minutes. Drain, reserve butter and set tomatoes aside.

1 tablespoon butter
1 medium potato, peeled and diced small
3 large fresh mushrooms, thinly sliced
1 medium zucchini, peeled and thinly sliced

• Melt butter in a large skillet over medium-low heat. Add reserved butter and diced potato. Cover and sauté until almost tender, about 20 minutes. Add mushrooms and zucchini. Sauté for another 5 minutes. Remove from heat.

5 eggs
⅓ teaspoon salt
1 dash black pepper
1 cup finely grated Swiss cheese
2 scallions, thinly sliced

• Crack eggs into a medium bowl. Using a whisk, beat eggs well. Add salt and black pepper, ¾ cup of the Swiss cheese, scallions and sautéed vegetables. Mix well.

2 tablespoons butter
2 tablespoons freshly grated Parmesan cheese
8 Sour Cream & Potato Tortillas *(recipe page 59),* **warmed, or Scallion Tortillas** *(recipe page 57),* **or Cottage Cheese Tortillas** *(recipe page 42)*

(continued on next page)

- Melt butter in a 10" skillet over low heat. Pour egg mixture in skillet and top with sun-dried tomatoes, Parmesan cheese and the remaining ¼ cup of Swiss cheese. Cook, uncovered, for 15 to 18 minutes. Remove from heat.
- Preheat oven to broil.
- Place the skillet in the oven, 2" below the broiler. Broil 30 to 60 seconds, or until the top is set.
- Loosen sides with a spatula. Cut the frittata into 16 wedges. Place 2 wedges *(in opposing directions)* on one side of each tortilla. Fold in half.

serves 4 to 6

Amazing Quiche with Hollandaise Sauce

When this Hollandaise is baked inside the quiche, the eggs become amazingly light and airy, a fact I discovered by accident. The effect is so dramatic that now I never make quiche without it!

Amazing Quiche

1	**teaspoon butter**
1	**cup thinly sliced mushrooms**
3	**scallions, thinly sliced**

• Melt butter in a small skillet over medium heat. Add sliced mushrooms and scallions. Sauté until tender, about 10 minutes. Cool to room temperature.

7	**eggs**
¼	**cup Hollandaise Sauce** *(recipe page 125),* **cold**
⅓	**cup sour cream**
¼	**cup milk**
¼	**teaspoon salt**
1	**dash white pepper**

• Preheat oven to 375°.

• In a medium bowl, combine eggs, Hollandaise Sauce, sour cream, milk, salt and white pepper. Mix well.

1	**9" Tortilla Pie Crust** *(recipe page 161)*
2	**cups finely grated Gruyere cheese**
4	**slices bacon, cooked crisp and crumbled**
1	**medium tomato, thinly sliced**

• Place cooled mushroom mixture in the bottom of the Tortilla Pie Crust. Sprinkle 1½ cups cheese over mushrooms. Pour eggs gently over the cheese. Sprinkle on remaining cheese and then top with crumbled bacon.

(continued on next page)

- Bake for 35 minutes, or until eggs are set.
- Top with a single layer of tomato slices. Return to the oven for 5 minutes, or until tomato slices are hot. Let stand 5 minutes on a wire rack before slicing.

serves 6 to 8

Hollandaise Sauce

1	**tablespoon fresh lemon juice**
½	**teaspoon dry sherry**
¼	**teaspoon dry hot mustard**

- Combine lemon juice, sherry and dry mustard. Set aside.

4	**egg yolks**
½	**cup cold butter, cut into thirds**

- Place the egg yolks and the first ⅓ of butter in a small saucepan. Place saucepan over a pan of boiling water *(or use a double boiler)*. Cook and stir until the butter is almost melted. Add the second ⅓ of butter. Stir until the butter is almost melted. Repeat with the last ⅓ of butter. Remove from heat.
- Immediately add the lemon mixture to the egg yolks, 1 teaspoon at a time, stirring well after each addition. Return to heat. Cook and stir until thickened enough to coat the spoon. *(Do not allow the sauce to boil or the egg yolks will curdle!)* Remove from heat. Transfer sauce to a small pitcher or serving dish. Use immediately or cover and refrigerate for later use.
- Reheat sauce by placing chilled Hollandaise Sauce in a small saucepan. Heat slowly over boiling water until warm, stirring occasionally, about 10 minutes. Serve immediately.

makes approximately ½ cup

Tortilla Stuffed Chile Peppers with Cashews & Avocado

This delicious recipe consists of mild anaheim chile peppers filled with a mixture of cream cheese and scallions, topped with cashews and fresh avocado slices, then wrapped in a tortilla and deep-fried until golden brown.

8 large anaheim chile peppers

- Remove tops and make a slice down one side of each pepper. Remove seeds and membrane. Rinse well. Steam peppers until tender, about 10 to 12 minutes. Cool on a wire rack.

1 8-ounce package cream cheese, softened
1½ tablespoons finely minced scallion
⅛ teaspoon black pepper
16 thin avocado slices *(about 1 medium avocado)*
½ cup whole cashews

- In a small bowl, combine the cream cheese, scallion and black pepper. Mix well.
- Spread ⅛ of the cream cheese mixture on the inside of 1 chile pepper. Tuck 2 avocado slices and 5 to 7 cashews on top of the cream cheese, inside of the pepper. Continue with the remaining 7 chile peppers.

dough for Sour Cream Tortillas *(recipe page 58),* **or Beer Tortillas** *(recipe page 32),* **or Traditional Flour Tortillas** *(recipe page 64)*
vegetable oil *(as needed)*

- Divide the dough into 8 pieces. Let rest 15 minutes.
- Roll out 1 piece of dough into a 5" x 10" rectangle. Place a stuffed pepper in the center of the rectangle, with the length of the pepper in the 10" direction. Gently fold the dough over the ends of the pepper *(toward the center)*. Then fold the dough over one side of the pepper, being sure to cover the opening of the chile pepper. Roll dough up over the pepper and seal edges by pinching them together.

(continued on next page)

- Preheat oven to 200°.
- Preheat 2" of vegetable oil in a tall 8" pan until hot, but not smoking, over medium-high heat.
- Deep-fry the peppers individually, until crisp and golden brown, turning only once. Roll out another piece of dough and prepare the next pepper while the first pepper is cooking. Place cooked peppers on a paper towel to drain. Keep warm in the oven. Continue with remaining peppers, adding more oil if needed.

½	**cup sour cream**
1	**avocado, peeled and pit removed, thinly sliced**
	salsa *(your favorite)*

- Serve immediately with sour cream, avocado slices and your favorite salsa.

Note: Freeze cooked chile peppers by wrapping them individually and placing in a sealed container. To reheat peppers, place on a baking sheet and cook in a preheated 375° oven until hot, about 20 to 25 minutes.

serves 6 to 8

Garden Vegetable Tortilla Pockets

This baked tortilla pocket contains a healthy, delicious blend of asparagus, red bell pepper, sliced sweet onion and sautéed mushrooms. Perfect for a light, evening meal, I usually prepare this dish in midsummer when fresh young vegetables are abundant.

8-10 fresh asparagus spears *(thin, if possible)*

- Steam asparagus until tender, about 8 to 10 minutes. Remove from heat and cool. Cut into 1" slices.

2 teaspoons butter
1 large red bell pepper, seeds and membrane removed, thinly sliced
1 medium sweet onion, thinly sliced
1 stalk celery, thinly sliced
12 medium mushrooms, thinly sliced

- Melt butter in a large skillet over medium heat. Add bell pepper, onion and celery. Sauté until tender, about 10 minutes. Add mushrooms and increase the heat slightly. Sauté until tender, about 5 more minutes. Drain off excess liquid. Cool to room temperature.

½ cup grated Gruyere cheese
salt and black pepper *(to taste)*

- In a medium bowl, combine steamed asparagus, bell pepper mixture and Gruyere cheese. Season with salt and black pepper. Refrigerate 1 hour.

dough for Scallion Tortillas *(recipe page 57)*, **or Avocado Tortillas** *(recipe page 31)*, **or Sour Cream Tortillas** *(recipe page 58)*

- Divide the dough into 8 pieces. Let rest 15 minutes.
- Preheat oven to 375°.

(continued on next page)

- On a lightly floured board, roll out 1 piece of dough into an 8" circle. Place ⅛ of the asparagus mixture in the center of the tortilla. Starting with the side closest to you, fold tortilla over just far enough to cover the asparagus mixture. Continue clockwise, folding up the other 3 sides, being sure that the dough overlaps on the top. Press the edges together with fingertips to seal. Place on an ungreased baking sheet. Continue with the remaining 7 pieces of dough.
- Using a toothpick, make 2 vent holes on the top of each tortilla pocket. *(For a fancier appearance, grated cheese can be sprinkled on top.)* Bake for 25 minutes, or until lightly browned.

serves 4 to 6

Sunny-Side Up Fried Rice Over Tortillas

This dish was inspired by one of my favorite Korean dishes, called Be Beam Bob. It makes a delicious and healthier change of pace for breakfast or lunch.

1 teaspoon peanut oil
½ cup finely sliced mushrooms

- Heat oil in a large skillet over medium heat. Sauté mushrooms until tender, about 10 minutes. Remove from heat and drain. Set mushrooms aside.

1½ tablespoons peanut oil
2 cups cooked rice

- Using the same skillet, heat oil over medium-high heat until very hot, but not smoking. Add rice to hot oil. Stir-fry until rice is well browned, about 5 minutes.

2 tablespoons soy sauce
2 teaspoons rice wine
⅛ teaspoon dry hot mustard
2 dashes garlic powder
1 dash ground ginger

- In a small bowl, combine soy sauce, rice wine, dry hot mustard, garlic powder and ground ginger. Add to browned rice and stir.

½ cup peas
6 fresh chives, finely minced

- To the browned rice, add sautéed mushrooms, peas and chives. Mix well. Keep warm over very low heat until ready for use.

(continued on next page)

4 **eggs, cooked sunny-side up**

4 **Traditional Flour Tortillas** *(recipe page 64),* **warmed, or Red Bell Pepper Tortillas** *(recipe page 52),* **or Oatmeal Tortillas** *(recipe page 47)*

soy sauce *(as needed)*

black pepper *(to taste)*

- Place 1/4 of the fried rice on top of each tortilla. Top each with a sunny-side up egg. Serve with soy sauce and black pepper.

serves 4

Sun-Dried Tomato Rice with Hidden Tortillas

This colorful dish is made with fresh whole kernel corn and sun-dried tomatoes that are plumped in a spicy butter mixture. The tortilla, hidden underneath, adds a surprise taste and texture.

- **3 tablespoons butter**
- **8 sun-dried tomatoes** *(not packed in oil),* **finely diced**
- **1 scallion, thinly sliced**
- **1 tablespoon diced green bell peppers**
- **1 teaspoon Worcestershire sauce**
- **2 dashes garlic powder**
- **1 dash cayenne pepper**

• Melt butter in a large saucepan, over medium heat until hot, but not browned. Add sun-dried tomatoes, scallion, green pepper, Worcestershire sauce, garlic powder and cayenne pepper. Mix well. Remove from heat, cover and let sit for 15 minutes.

- **1 large ear of corn, cooked**
- **3 cups cooked rice, hot**
- **4 "Corn" Tortillas with Caramelized Onion** *(recipe page 40),* **warmed, or Yogurt Tortillas** *(recipe page 66),* **or Whole Wheat Tortillas** *(recipe page 65)*
- **1 cup grated Swiss cheese**

• Cut corn off the cob. Add to tomato mixture and stir.

• Fluff hot rice with a fork and add to corn and tomato mixture. Stir gently.

• Place rice in the center of each tortilla and cover completely. Top with grated Swiss cheese.

serves 4

Soft Tostada

These soft and chewy tortillas are piled high with frijoles, plum tomatoes, lettuce, Cheddar cheese, sour cream and green scallions. They're nearly impossible to pick up with your fingers, so a knife and fork are a true necessity.

2⅔	**cups Spicy Frijoles** *(recipe page 101),* **hot**
8	**5" Steamed Tortillas** *(recipe page 62),* **warmed**
4	**plum tomatoes, thinly sliced**
2	**cups shredded iceberg lettuce**
2	**cups finely grated Cheddar cheese**
¾	**cup sour cream**
2	**scallions, thinly sliced**
	salsa *(your favorite)*

- Spread ⅓ cup Spicy Frijoles over each tortilla. Top each with several slices of tomato and ¼ cup of shredded lettuce. Sprinkle ¼ cup grated Cheddar cheese over the lettuce and top with a dollop of sour cream. Sprinkle each tostada with a few scallions. Serve with your favorite salsa.

serves 4 to 6

Macaroni & Three Cheese Pie

Tender macaroni, a rich cream sauce, and layers of Parmesan and sharp Cheddar cheese are baked to perfection inside a crispy Tortilla Pie Crust. On hurried evenings I make this dish without the crust, in a small casserole dish.

1 9" Tortilla Pie Crust *(recipe page 161)*

- Prepare crust. Cover with a clean dish towel and set aside.

2½ tablespoons butter
3 tablespoons white flour
1½ cups milk
½ teaspoon salt
1 dash cayenne pepper
3 ounces cream cheese, softened

- Preheat oven to 375°.
- Melt butter in a small saucepan over medium-low heat. Add flour. Cook and stir 1 minute.
- Add milk, salt and cayenne pepper. Cook and stir until thickened and bubbly, about 10 minutes. Remove from heat.
- Add cream cheese. Using a whisk, blend well.

1½ cups elbow macaroni, cooked al dente and drained
2 cups grated sharp Cheddar cheese
½ cup freshly grated Parmesan cheese

- Place half of the macaroni, evenly, in the bottom of the Tortilla Pie Crust. Pour half of the sauce over macaroni. Top with ¼ cup Parmesan cheese and 1 cup sharp Cheddar cheese. Repeat layers with the remaining ingredients.
- Bake for 25 to 30 minutes, or until crust is lightly browned. Let sit 10 minutes before slicing.

serves 6

Asiago Fettucine

Asiago cheese has a rich, Parmesan-like flavor and a smooth texture when melted, which makes this pasta dish especially rich and flavorful. It's our family's favorite "fast food"!

16 **5" Lemon Spinach Tortillas** *(recipe page 46),* **or Sun-Dried Tomato Tortillas** *(recipe page 61),* **or Traditional Flour Tortillas** *(recipe page 64)*

- Preheat oven to 350°.
- Wrap tortillas in foil. Place in the oven for 10 to 15 minutes, or until warm.

8 **ounces fettucine** *(fresh, if possible),* **cooked al dente and drained**
5 **ounces Asiago cheese, finely grated**
2 **tablespoons minced fresh chives**
1/8 **teaspoon black pepper**
2 **cups Cream Sauce** *(recipe page 139),* **hot**

- Toss hot fettucine with Asiago cheese, chives and black pepper. Pour Cream Sauce over pasta. Toss gently.

4 **sprigs fresh parsley**
finely grated Asiago cheese *(as needed)*
black pepper *(to taste)*

- Place each tortilla on an individual plate. Place the pasta on top. Garnish each dish with fresh parsley.
- Serve with plenty of grated cheese and black pepper.

serves 4

Apricot Prawns with Tortillas & Tarragon Cream Sauce

This dish was inspired by a wonderful meal I once had at the Seven Gables Restaurant in Olympia, Washington. The sauce is fantastic, with just a hint of rich Gorgonzola cheese and savory tarragon.

Apricot Prawns

- 1 **teaspoon butter**
- 3 **scallions, thinly sliced**
- ½ **medium red bell pepper, seeds and membrane removed, thinly sliced**
- ½ **stalk celery, thinly sliced**

• Melt butter in a large skillet over medium-high heat. Add scallions, bell pepper and celery. Sauté until tender, about 10 minutes.

- 2 **tablespoons brut Champagne**
- 1 **pound prawns** *(or large shrimp),* **shelled and deveined**
- ¼ **cup crumbled Gorgonzola cheese**
- 1 **cup Tarragon Cream Sauce** *(recipe page 137),* **hot**
- **salt and black pepper** *(to taste)*
- 4 **Cream Cheese Tortillas** *(recipe page 43),* **warmed, or Red Bell Pepper Tortillas** *(recipe page 52),* **or Sour Cream Tortillas** *(recipe page 58)*

• Add Champagne to bell pepper mixture. Add prawns. Sauté until pink and loosely curled, about 2 to 3 minutes.

• Sprinkle cheese over prawns and vegetables.

• Add Tarragon Cream Sauce and mix gently. Season with salt and black pepper.

• Immediately place a generous amount of Apricot Prawns in the center of each tortilla.

serves 4

Tarragon Cream Sauce

¾	**cup water**
6	**dried apricot halves, finely diced**

- Place water in a small saucepan and bring to a boil over medium heat. Add dried apricots. Simmer until liquid is reduced to about 2 tablespoons. Using a small, finely meshed strainer, strain juice into a medium saucepan. Discard apricot pieces.

1	**cup heavy cream**
2	**tablespoons milk**
2	**teaspoons dried parsley**
¼	**teaspoon white pepper**
⅛	**teaspoon salt**
1	**dash dried tarragon**
2	**egg yolks, lightly beaten**
2	**dried apricot halves, thinly sliced**

- To the strained juice add cream, milk, parsley, white pepper, salt and tarragon. Heat to simmering over low heat.
- Add several tablespoons of cream mixture to the egg yolks and mix quickly. Add egg yolks back to the cream. Continue cooking until mixture is slightly thickened, enough to lightly coat the spoon. *(Do not allow the sauce to boil or the egg yolks will curdle.)* Remove from heat. Add sliced apricots and stir.

makes 1 cup

Chicken & Chive Filled Tortillas with Cream Sauce

Tortillas filled with chicken and fresh chives are individually wrapped in parchment paper and then heated in the oven. Accompanied by a rich cream sauce and toasted almonds, this dish tastes as good as it looks.

Chicken & Chive Filled Tortillas

1	**teaspoon butter**
1	**pound mushrooms, thinly sliced**

• Melt butter in a medium skillet over medium-high heat. Add mushrooms and sauté until tender, about 10 minutes. Drain.

2	**whole chicken breasts, cooked, skin and bones removed, and cubed**
1/4	**cup finely minced fresh chives**
1	**cup sour cream**
1	**dash cayenne pepper**
1 1/2	**cups grated Provolone cheese**
	salt *(to taste)*
	black pepper *(to taste)*

• In a large bowl, combine sautéed mushrooms, chicken, chives, sour cream and cayenne pepper. Mix well. Add cheese and mix gently, until well combined. Season with salt and black pepper.

8	**Red Bell Pepper Tortillas** *(recipe page 52),* **or Sourdough Tortillas** *(recipe page 60),* **or Potato & Yogurt Tortillas** *(recipe page 51)*
2	**cups Cream Sauce** *(recipe page 139),* **hot**
1/2	**cup slivered almonds, toasted**

(continued on next page)

- Preheat oven to 375°.
- Place about ½ cup of the chicken mixture on one side of a tortilla. Starting on the filled side, roll up the tortilla. Wrap the filled tortilla in parchment paper. Continue with the remaining 7 tortillas. Place wrapped tortillas in a 13" x 9" pan and bake for 15 minutes, or until hot. Remove the parchment paper.
- Ladle the Cream Sauce on top of each serving and sprinkle with toasted almonds.

serves 4 to 6

Cream Sauce

4 **large egg yolks, lightly beaten**

- Place lightly beaten egg yolks in a small glass bowl and set aside.

2 **cups half & half**
salt *(to taste)*
white pepper *(to taste)*

- In a small saucepan, heat half & half over low heat until bubbles form on the edge of the pan.
- Pour a small amount of hot half & half into the egg yolks. Whisk quickly to combine, and immediately return the mixture to the saucepan. Cook and stir over very low heat for 3 to 4 minutes, or until thickened enough to coat the spoon. *(Do not let the mixture boil or the egg yolks will curdle.)*
- Remove from heat. Season with salt and white pepper.

makes 2 cups

Mexican-Style Chicken Steamed Buns

A great alternative to deep-frying, these steamed "chimichangas" are filled with shredded chicken, minced yellow chile peppers and diced Granny Smith apples.

2	**cups cooked and finely shredded chicken, skin removed**
½	**cup diced Granny Smith apples**
¼	**cup finely grated Asiago cheese**
2½	**tablespoons minced fresh chives**
2½	**teaspoons minced yellow chile pepper, seeds and membrane removed**
1	**dash garlic powder**
1	**dash salt**
⅛	**teaspoon black pepper**

- In a medium bowl, combine chicken, diced apples and cheese. Add chives, minced yellow chile pepper and spices. Mix well. Cover and refrigerate until ready for use.

dough for Cottage Cheese Tortillas *(recipe page 42),* **or Whole Wheat Tortillas** *(recipe page 65),* **or Butter Tortillas** *(recipe page 35)*

- Divide the dough into 8 equal pieces. Let rest 15 minutes.

- On a lightly floured board, roll 1 piece of dough into an 8" circle. Place ½ cup filling on one side of the rolled tortilla. Fold the left and the right sides of the tortilla inward *(the edges should not meet in the center)*. Starting from the filled side, roll up the tortilla. Pinch well to seal the edges. Continue with the remaining 7 pieces of dough.

	water *(as needed)*
1	**corn husk** *(for steaming)*

- Preheat a covered 8" skillet over medium heat, containing a flat vegetable steamer and ½" depth of water, until hot and steamy. Line the steamer with the corn husk to prevent the tortillas from sticking.

(continued on next page)

- Preheat oven to 200°.
- Steam 2 of the filled tortillas in the preheated skillet, covered, for 3 minutes.
- Using 2 spatulas, carefully turn each tortilla over. Replace the cover and continue to steam for another 3 minutes. Remove cooked tortillas and place them on a wire rack in the oven to keep warm. Continue steaming the remaining 6 filled tortillas, 2 at a time. *(Check the water level in the skillet often, adding hot water as necessary.)*

1¼ cups Guacamole *(recipe page 93)*
1 cup sour cream
½ cup whole cashews

- Serve the steamed buns with a dollop of both the Guacamole and sour cream. Garnish each with a few whole cashews.

serves 6

Orange Chicken Tortilla Pockets with Raisins

A beautiful and delicately flavored dish, these flower-shaped tortilla pockets are filled with shredded chicken, tangy orange zest and sweet, plump raisins.

- **1 tablespoon butter**
- **2½ tablespoons minced shallots**
- **½ cup raisins**
- **¼ teaspoon freshly grated orange zest**
- **1½ tablespoons freshly squeezed orange juice**
- **1 teaspoon dried chervil**
- **¼ teaspoon black pepper**
- **2 cups cooked and shredded chicken, skin removed**

• Melt butter in a medium saucepan over low heat. Add shallots and sauté 1 minute. Add raisins, orange zest, orange juice, chervil and black pepper. Mix well. Cover and cook over very low heat until raisins are plumped, about 5 minutes. Remove from heat.

• Add shredded chicken and mix well. Chill.

- **dough for Yogurt Tortillas** *(recipe page 66)*, **or Parmesan Cheese Tortillas** *(recipe page 49)*, **or Cream Cheese Tortillas** *(recipe page 43)*
- **1 egg yolk, slightly beaten**
- **1 cup Strong Brown Chicken Stock** *(recipe page 162)*, **heated**
- **12 fresh orange slices**
- **6 sprigs of parsley**

• Divide dough into 6 pieces. Let rest 15 minutes.

• Preheat oven to 375°.

(continued on next page)

- On a lightly floured board, roll 1 piece of dough into an 8" circle. Place 1/6 of the chicken filling in the center of the rolled tortilla. Lift 2 *(out of 3)* edges of the tortilla, matching the inside edges together. Pinch well. Lift the remaining side, matching the inside edges on both sides, and pinch well to create a "Y" shaped seam. *(Be sure to allow excess air to escape before pinching the final seam.)* Working clockwise, fold each of the 3 points back into the center, pinching well after each.
- Place the filled tortilla on an ungreased baking sheet. Continue rolling and filling the remaining 5 pieces of dough.
- Lightly brush each tortilla pocket with the beaten egg yolk.
- Bake for 30 minutes, or until lightly browned.
- Serve each tortilla pocket with a small bowl of warm Strong Brown Chicken Stock. Garnish with fresh orange slices and a sprig of parsley.

serves 4 to 6

Chicken Chimichangas

These mouth-watering chimichangas are filled with chicken, dried cranberries and almonds, then deep-fried until golden brown. Just prior to serving, they are drizzled with a spicy brown sauce and crowned with a dollop of sour cream. Chimichangas can be made in advance and stored in the freezer until ready for use.

- 3 **whole chicken breasts, cooked, skin and bones removed, shredded**
- 3 **scallions, thinly sliced**
- ½ **cup dried cranberries** *(or raisins)*
- ½ **cup slivered almonds, toasted**
- **salt** *(to taste)*
- **black pepper** *(to taste)*

• Combine chicken, scallions, cranberries and almonds. Season with salt and black pepper. Mix well.

- 1 **cup Brown Sauce II** *(recipe page 166)*
- 1 **dash ground coriander**
- ⅛ **teaspoon ground cumin**
- **salt** *(to taste)*
- **black pepper** *(to taste)*

• Heat Brown Sauce II in a small saucepan over low heat. Add coriander and cumin, and stir. Season with salt and black pepper. Keep warm until ready for use, stirring occasionally.

- **dough for Parmesan Cheese Tortillas** *(recipe page 49),* **or Risen (Yeast) Tortillas** *(recipe page 54),* **or Applesauce Tortillas** *(recipe page 30)*
- **vegetable oil** *(as needed)*
- **sour cream** *(as needed)*

• Divide dough into 8 pieces. Let rest 15 minutes.

(continued on next page)

- On a lightly floured board, roll 1 piece of dough into an 8" circle. Place ⅓ cup of the chicken mixture on one side of the rolled tortilla. Fold the left and the right sides of the tortilla inward *(the edges will not meet in the center)*. Starting from the filled side, roll up the tortilla. Pinch well to seal edges. Slightly flatten the sealed chimichanga.
- Preheat oven to 200°.
- Place vegetable oil, 1" deep, in a tall 8" skillet. Preheat oil over medium heat until very hot, but not smoking.
- Deep-fry the chimichanga in the preheated oil until golden brown, turning only once, about 60 seconds per side. Meanwhile, prepare the next chimichanga.
- Place the cooked chimichangas in an oven-proof serving dish lined with a paper towel. Keep warm in oven until serving.
- Serve chimichangas on individual plates, each topped with ⅛ cup seasoned brown sauce and a dollop of sour cream.

Note: To reheat chimichangas, place on an ungreased baking sheet and bake in a preheated 375° oven for 15 minutes, or until hot. Allow 30 to 35 minutes for frozen chimichangas.

serves 4 to 6

Marinated Halibut Tacos

My introduction to fish tacos was in Southern California some years ago, and although appreciative of the concept, I objected to the oily taste of deep-fried cod. Therefore, my version is prepared with fresh halibut filets, marinated in red jalapeño jelly and butter, then grilled to perfection.

- 2 **tablespoons butter, melted**
- 2 **tablespoons red jalapeño jelly** *(The El Paso Chile Co., if possible)*
- 1 **teaspoon minced fresh lemon balm**
- 1 **teaspoon minced fresh chives**
- 1 **dash salt**
- 1 **dash white pepper**

• In a small bowl, combine melted butter, red jalapeño jelly, lemon balm, chives, salt and white pepper. Mix well.

- 1 **pound Alaskan halibut filets**

• Place halibut in a 9"x 9" baking dish. Brush both sides of the fish with the red jalapeño marinade. Cover and refrigerate 15 minutes.

• Grill the fillets over hot coals for 5 minutes on each side, or until fish is tender and flakes with a fork. Slice into ½" wide pieces.

- 6 **Jalapeño Tortillas** *(recipe page 44),* **warmed, or Romano Cheese & Chive Tortillas** *(recipe page 56),* **or Sourdough Tortillas** *(recipe page 60)*
- 1 **large tomato, finely diced**
- 2 **cups finely shredded iceberg lettuce**
- 1 **cup sour cream**
- ½ **cup red jalapeño jelly** *(or as needed)*

• Place several pieces of grilled halibut on one side of each tortilla. Top with diced tomato, lettuce and a dollop of sour cream. Fold the tortilla over. Serve with a small dish of red jalapeño jelly on the side.

serves 4

Tortilla Buffet

Let your guests create their own masterpiece burritos with this colorful buffet! The preparations are made in advance so you can relax and enjoy yourself as you entertain. With such a wide variety of choices, even less adventuresome eaters will be satisfied.

1½ cups coarsely grated Cheddar cheese
1½ cups coarsely grated Monterey Jack cheese
2 cups shredded iceberg lettuce
2 large tomatoes, finely diced
1 cup sliced black olives
1 cup finely diced green chile peppers

- Place each ingredient in individual serving dishes. Cover and refrigerate until ready to serve.

20 Cheddar Cheese Tortillas *(recipe page 39),* **warmed, or Avocado Tortillas** *(recipe page 31),* **or Corn Tortillas with Cheese & Chives** *(recipe page 41),* **or a combination of these tortillas**
3 cups Spicy Frijoles *(recipe page 101),* **warmed**
1½ pounds cooked and shredded beef, warmed
1½ pounds cooked and shredded chicken, warmed

- Place tortillas, Spicy Frijoles, beef and chicken on serving plates. If possible, place them over a warmer, on the buffet table.

2 avocados, peeled and pitted, thinly sliced
½ cup raisins
½ cup dried cherries *(unsweetened)*
½ cup slivered almonds, toasted
1½ cups sour cream
1 cup tomato salsa *(your favorite)*
1 cup cactus salsa *(The El Paso Chile Co., if possible)*

- Place the above ingredients in individual serving dishes and set on the buffet table.

serves 8 to 10

Tiny Greek Tortilla "Pizzas"

Ground lamb, scallions, garlic and tomato paste are encased in a risen tortilla and then topped with grated Myzhopa cheese. Myzhopa is a Greek sheep cheese, which becomes beautifully crisp when baked. These tiny, five-inch, Greek "pizzas" are popular with both children and adults.

1½	**pounds ground lamb**
5	**scallions, thinly sliced**
1	**clove garlic, very finely minced**
⅓	**cup pine nuts, toasted**
1	**tablespoon minced fresh parsley**
4	**ounces tomato paste**
1	**tablespoon fresh lemon juice**
2	**dashes Tabasco sauce**
1¼	**teaspoons sugar**
¾	**teaspoon allspice**
1	**teaspoon salt**
½	**teaspoon black pepper**

- In a large skillet, brown the ground lamb over medium-high heat, stirring often. Remove from heat and drain well.
- Add scallions, garlic, pine nuts, parsley, tomato paste, lemon juice, Tabasco sauce, sugar and spices. Mix well.

dough for Risen (Yeast) Tortillas *(recipe page 54)* **or Sourdough Tortillas** *(recipe page 60)*

- Divide dough into 8 pieces. Let rest 15 minutes.
- Preheat oven to 450°.

(continued on next page)

- Roll out 1 piece of dough into an 8" circle. Place 1⁄8 of the lamb mixture in the center and spread it into a 5" circle. Starting on one side and working around the circle clockwise, fold one edge of the dough over the meat mixture. Move 1 1⁄2" around the circle and fold up the next edge. Be sure to pinch the dough together where it overlaps. Continue folding and pinching all the way around the circle. *(When finished, the center 3" will still be exposed.)* Lift the filled tortilla carefully and place on a lightly greased baking sheet. Continue rolling and filling the remaining 7 pieces of dough.

1⁄3	**cup finely grated Myzhopa cheese**
8	**sprigs fresh parsley**
	sour cream *(as needed)*
	salsa *(your favorite)*

- Sprinkle about 1 teaspoon Myzhopa cheese over the exposed meat.
- Bake for 10 to 12 minutes, or until golden brown.
- Garnish with a sprig of fresh parsley in the center of each tortilla. Serve with sour cream and your favorite salsa.

serves 8

Shredded Beef Tortilla Pockets

These delicious baked tortillas are filled with shredded beef and fresh mushrooms, then decorated with sliced Provolone cheese on top. I often make these pocket sandwiches and then freeze them for my husband's lunches ..... a gesture he always appreciates!

1 teaspoon butter
¼ pound fresh mushrooms, thinly sliced
2 scallions, thinly sliced

- Melt butter in a small skillet over medium heat. Sauté mushrooms and scallions until tender, about 5 minutes. Remove from heat and drain well.

2 cups cooked and shredded beef
¼ cup freshly grated Parmesan cheese
⅓ cup catsup
2 tablespoons Worcestershire sauce
salt and black pepper *(to taste)*

- In a medium bowl, combine beef, Parmesan cheese, catsup, Worcestershire sauce and sautéed mushrooms. Mix well. Season with salt and black pepper.

dough for Potato & Yogurt Tortillas *(recipe page 51),* **or Risen (Yeast) Tortillas** *(recipe page 54),* **or Cottage Cheese Tortillas** *(recipe page 42)*

- Divide dough into 10 pieces. Let rest 15 minutes.
- Preheat oven to 375°.
- On a lightly floured board, roll out 1 piece of dough into an 8" circle. Place ¼ cup beef mixture in the center of the tortilla. Starting with the side closest to you, fold the edge of the tortilla over, just far enough to cover beef mixture. Continue clockwise, folding up the other 3 sides, being sure that the dough overlaps on the top. Pinch well to seal edges. Place on an ungreased baking sheet. Continue with the remaining 9 pieces of dough.

(continued on next page)

5 **slices Provolone cheese, each cut in half**
sour cream *(as needed)*
salsa *(your favorite)*

- Place a half slice of cheese on top of each pocket.
- Bake for 30 minutes, or until golden brown.
- Serve with sour cream and your favorite salsa.

serves 6 to 8

Chipotle Chile Taco with Corn

Hidden inside fresh tortillas is a spicy bean chile made with dried chipotle chile peppers, whole kernel corn and lean ground beef.

1	**tablespoon butter**
1 ¼	**cups coarsely chopped sweet onion**
¼	**cup minced yellow bell pepper**
1	**clove garlic, finely minced**

- Melt butter in a large saucepan over medium heat. Add onion, bell pepper and garlic. Sauté until tender, about 10 minutes.

1	**14-ounce can tomato sauce**
1	**cup beer**
½	**cup water**
2	**dried chipotle chile peppers**
2	**teaspoons dried parsley**
2	**teaspoons finely minced fresh basil**
¾	**teaspoon ground cumin**
½	**teaspoon maple sugar**
½	**teaspoon chile powder**
¼	**teaspoon dried oregano**
⅓	**teaspoon black pepper**
2	**dashes Tabasco sauce** *(or to taste)*

- Add tomato sauce, beer, water and dried chipotle chile peppers. Stir. Add spices. Stir well. Simmer gently for 1 hour. Remove chipotle peppers and discard.

1 ½	**pounds lean ground beef**
1	**16-ounce can light red kidney beans, drained**
1	**cup corn kernels**
4	**tablespoons tomato paste**
1	**dash salt**
	water *(as needed)*

(continued on next page)

• In a large skillet, over medium heat, brown ground beef. Drain well.

• To the simmered sauce, add beef, kidney beans, corn, tomato paste and salt. Simmer 1 hour, adding ½ to 1 cup water if chile becomes too thick.

8 Beer Tortillas *(recipe page 32),* **warmed, or Scallion Tortillas** *(recipe page 57),* **or Butter Tortillas** *(recipe page 35)*
2 cups grated sharp Cheddar cheese
2 cups finely shredded iceberg lettuce
1 cup finely diced tomato
1 cup sour cream

• Place chile on one side of each tortilla. Top with cheese, lettuce, tomato and a dollop of sour cream. Fold tortilla in half over filling. Top with a little more chile and a sprinkle of cheese.

serves 4 to 6

Grilled Skewers of Filet Mignon with a Spirited Horseradish Sauce

Each grilled skewer is laid on top of a fresh tortilla, drizzled with tangy horseradish sauce, then topped with pumpkin seeds and fresh mint leaves. Provide plenty of freshly grated horseradish and an extra plate for discarded skewers.

Grilled Skewers of Filet Mignon

2 **pounds filet mignon, thinly sliced**
2 **tablespoons butter, melted**
1 **clove garlic, finely minced**
3 **dashes freshly ground green peppercorns**

- Arrange slices of beef, loosely, on eight 10" bamboo skewers.
- Combine melted butter, garlic and ground green peppercorns. Brush both sides of the beef slices with the butter mixture. Grill over very hot coals until medium-rare, about 3 to 4 minutes on each side.

8 **Cottage Cheese Tortillas** *(recipe page 42),* **warmed, or Romano Cheese & Chive Tortillas** *(recipe page 56),* **or Potato Tortillas** *(recipe page 50)*
1 **cup Spirited Horseradish Sauce** *(recipe page 155)*
⅓ **cup pepitas** *(pumpkin seeds)*
24 **small fresh mint leaves**
peeled and freshly grated horseradish *(as needed)*

- Place 1 beef skewer in the center of each tortilla. Top with a generous amount of Spirited Horseradish Sauce and several pepitas. Garnish each with 3 mint leaves, arranged like a small flower.

serves 4

Spirited Horseradish Sauce

1 cup sour cream
2 tablespoons milk
2 tablespoons minced fresh chives
2 tablespoons butter, softened
4 tablespoons freshly grated horseradish, peeled
1 teaspoon tarragon vinegar
½ teaspoon dried chervil

- In a small bowl, combine sour cream, milk, chives, butter, horseradish, tarragon vinegar and chervil. Mix well. Cover and refrigerate 1 hour, or until ready to use.

makes 1 cup

Steak Fajitas

Steak Fajitas are made with marinated and grilled spencer steaks, sweet red bell peppers and tender onions. I usually serve them with a generous helping of rice and refried beans, garnished with fresh apple slices.

1/4	**cup soy sauce**
1	**tablespoon vegetable oil**
1	**teaspoon Tabasco sauce**
1	**clove garlic, finely minced**
	juice from 1 lime
2	**12-ounce spencer steaks**

- In a 9" x 9" baking dish, combine soy sauce, vegetable oil, Tabasco sauce, garlic and lime juice. Add steaks and marinate in the refrigerator for 1 hour.
- Grill marinated steaks over hot coals, until medium-rare. Cool and slice thinly.

2	**tablespoons vegetable oil**
2	**red bell peppers, seeds and membrane removed, thinly sliced**
1	**medium onion, finely chopped**
	salt and black pepper *(to taste)*

- Heat oil in a very large skillet *(or wok)* over medium-high heat. Add red bell peppers and onion. Sauté until tender, about 5 to 6 minutes. Add sliced beef and sauté until hot, about 3 minutes. Season with salt and black pepper.

6	**Black Olive and Sour Cream Tortillas** *(recipe page 33)*, **warmed, or Cheddar Cheese Tortillas** *(recipe page 39)*, **or Lemon Spinach Tortillas** *(recipe page 46)*
	sour cream *(as needed)*
	salsa *(your favorite)*
1	**apple, thinly sliced**

- Place fajita mixture on one side of each tortilla. Fold in half. Serve with sour cream and your favorite salsa. Garnish with several apple slices.

serves 4 to 6

Tortilla Poor Boy Sandwich

As colorful as it is tasty, this open-face tortilla sandwich is reminiscent of the famous New Orleans Poor Boy. It is made with tender shredded beef smothered in brown sauce, then topped with lots of fried red cabbage.

3	**tablespoons butter**
3	**tablespoons white flour**
1/8	**teaspoon salt**
1	**dash black pepper**
1 1/2	**cups Rich & Spicy Beef Stock** *(recipe page 163)*

- Melt butter in a medium saucepan over medium-low heat. Add flour. Cook and stir 1 minute. Add salt, black pepper and Rich & Spicy Beef Stock. Cook and stir until thickened and bubbly, about 10 minutes. Remove from heat.

1	**tablespoon butter**
3	**1/4" thick slices red cabbage, separated**
2	**tablespoons freshly grated Parmesan cheese**
1	**dash garlic powder**
2	**dashes salt**

- Melt butter in a large skillet over medium-high heat. Add sliced cabbage. Stir-fry until tender, about 5 minutes.
- Add Parmesan cheese, garlic powder and salt. Stir-fry another 2 minutes. Remove from heat.

	Dijon mustard *(as needed)*
4	**Sourdough Tortillas** *(recipe page 60),* **warmed, or Buttermilk & Potato Tortillas** *(recipe page 37),* **or Yogurt Soda Tortillas** *(recipe page 67)*
3	**cups cooked and shredded beef, warmed**
12	**black olives stuffed with cream cheese**

- Spread a small amount of Dijon mustard on top of each tortilla. Top each with 3/4 cup warmed shredded beef and a liberal amount of brown sauce. Place fried cabbage in the center of each tortilla. Garnish with several stuffed black olives.

serves 4

Significant Others

Vermouth Roasted Garlic

By roasting garlic very slowly in olive oil and vermouth, and then mashing the cloves, an incredibly flavorful paste is formed, without a lingering aftertaste. I find it to be an excellent replacement for raw or sautéed garlic.

2	**heads fresh garlic**
¼	**cup vermouth**
3	**tablespoons olive oil**
⅛	**teaspoon black pepper**

- Preheat oven to 300°.
- Remove papery skin from the exterior of garlic heads. Place both heads of garlic in a small glass baking dish *(with lid),* lined with aluminum foil. Pour vermouth and olive oil over garlic. Sprinkle with black pepper.
- Cover and bake 1½ hours. Cool to room temperature.
- Remove garlic by gently squeezing the cloves, 1 at a time, into a sealable container. Using a fork *(or your fingers)*, mash the garlic into a paste.
- Refrigerate until ready for use.

makes approximately ⅛ cup garlic paste

Tortilla Pie Crust

This crispy pie crust is much lower in calories than traditional crusts. Use it for quiches or other savory fillings.

- ¾ **cup white flour**
- ¼ **teaspoon salt**
- ½ **teaspoon baking powder**
- 1 **dash cayenne pepper**

• Sift the dry ingredients into a small bowl.

- 1 **tablespoon butter, softened**

• Cut the butter into the flour until the mixture resembles coarse meal.

- ¼ **cup cottage cheese** *(small curd)*
- 2 **tablespoons water**

• Combine the cottage cheese and water, and stir.

• Add the cottage cheese mixture to the flour mixture all at once. Mix well. Gather the dough into a ball. *(The dough should be soft and slightly sticky.)* Wrap dough in lightly floured wax paper and refrigerate until medium-firm, about 30 to 45 minutes.

• Between lightly floured sheets of wax paper, roll the dough into a circle that is large enough to overlap a 9" pie pan, about 15" to 16" in diameter. Peel off the top sheet of wax paper. Place the pie pan upside down over the dough and invert. Peel off the second piece of wax paper. Press the dough gently to remove air spaces on the bottom and sides. Trim the dough even with the rim. Fold ¼" of the dough underneath, making a smooth edge. Press firmly to seal.

- 1 **teaspoon butter, softened**

• Lightly rub the dough with butter before filling.

makes one 9" pie crust

Strong Brown Chicken Stock

This dark brown, very flavorful chicken stock is made with onions, celery, carrots, roasted garlic and minced jalapeño chile peppers. It may take several hours longer to simmer than most other chicken stocks, but it is the best one I've ever tasted!

- 1 **3-4 pound whole chicken, giblets removed and well rinsed**
- 3 **quarts water** *(or as needed)*
- 2 **medium onions, thickly sliced**
- 4 **ribs celery with leaves, coarsely chopped**
- 4 **carrots** *(with peel),* **quartered**
- 1 **head Vermouth Roasted Garlic** *(recipe page 160),* **or 2 cloves fresh minced garlic**
- 1 **tablespoon minced fresh basil**
- ¼ **teaspoon dried minced jalapeño chile pepper** *(or 1 teaspoon fresh minced)*

- Place chicken in a large soup pot. Add water until chicken is covered. Add onion, celery, carrots, garlic, basil and jalapeño chile pepper. Cover and simmer over very low heat for 2 to 2½ hours, or until chicken is tender. Remove from heat and cool.
- Carefully remove chicken from the broth and reserve meat for later use. Using a large, finely meshed strainer, strain broth into a large soup pan and discard the vegetables.
- Simmer strained broth over low heat for about 2 hours, or until the broth is reduced to 4 cups. Remove from heat and cool.
- Pour broth into 2 sealable storage containers and refrigerate until cold.
- Skim the fat and discard. *(The broth will be quite gelatinous)*. Use immediately or store frozen for future use.

makes 1 quart

Rich & Spicy Beef Stock

Fresh vegetables and a variety of spices contribute to the full-bodied flavor of this beef stock. It is an excellent base for most soups and sauces.

1½ tablespoons olive oil
4 pounds chuck steak, thick cut

- In a large dutch oven, heat oil over medium heat. Sear chuck steak on each side until well browned.

1 quart water
1 large carrot *(with peel),* **quartered**
2 large scallions, sliced
½ medium red bell pepper, seeds and membrane removed, thinly sliced
2 cloves garlic, minced
2 ounces tomato paste
1 teaspoon fresh lemon juice
½ teaspoon dried chervil
¼ teaspoon ground cumin
¼ teaspoon dried minced jalapeño chile pepper *(or 1 teaspoon fresh minced)*
⅛ teaspoon ground coriander
⅛ teaspoon black pepper

- Preheat oven to 350°.
- Pour water over meat. Add carrot, scallions, red bell pepper, garlic, tomato paste, lemon juice, chervil, cumin, jalapeño chile pepper, coriander and black pepper. Cover and braise in the oven for 4½ hours, or until meat is very tender.
- Carefully remove chuck steak from the broth and reserve meat for later use. Using a large, finely meshed strainer, strain broth into a sealable container. Discard vegetables. Refrigerate until cold.
- Skim the fat and discard. Use immediately or store frozen for future use.

makes approximately 3 cups

Brown Sauce I

The key to the success of this sauce is the inclusion of an extremely rich, flavorful stock. Although the ingredients take only minutes to combine, they must simmer for at least four hours in the oven. The sauce may be prepared ahead of time and will age gracefully for several days in the refrigerator.

- ¼ **cup white flour**
- ⅛ **teaspoon black pepper**
- 2 **pounds chuck steak**
- 2 **tablespoons vegetable oil**

• Combine flour and black pepper. Rub flour onto meat until thoroughly covered.

• Heat oil in a large skillet over medium heat until hot. Sear chuck steak in hot oil until lightly browned on both sides. Remove from heat.

- 2 **carrots** *(with peel),* **quartered**
- ½ **medium onion, quartered**
- ½ **cup diced tomato**
- 1 **bay leaf**
- 1 **dash cayenne pepper**
- 1 **quart water**

• Preheat oven to 325°.

• Place meat in a large, oven-proof soup pot *(or dutch oven)*. Add carrot, onion, tomato, bay leaf, cayenne pepper and water. Cover and cook in the oven until the meat is tender, about 4 hours. Cool to room temperature.

• Carefully remove chuck steak from beef stock and reserve meat for later use. Using a large, finely meshed strainer, strain beef stock into a sealable container, discarding vegetables.

• Refrigerate until cold. Skim the fat and discard.

(continued on next page)

water *(as needed)*
2¾ **tablespoons cornstarch**
salt *(to taste)*
black pepper *(to taste)*

- Place beef stock in a four-cup measuring cup. Add enough water to the stock to equal 3 cups. Add the cornstarch and stir until dissolved.
- Pour beef stock into a medium saucepan. Cook and stir over medium-low heat until boiling. Boil 1 minute. Remove sauce from the heat.
- Season with salt and black pepper. Use immediately or refrigerate until ready for use.

makes 3 cups

Brown Sauce II

I like to make the beef stock for this sauce on a cold day because it warms the kitchen and fills the house with a wonderful aroma. The ingredients of mushrooms, celery and bacon add a delicious, rich flavor.

3 slices bacon

- Cook bacon in a large skillet over medium-low heat until crisp, about 15 minutes. Remove bacon from pan and set aside. Reserve bacon grease for searing the chuck steak.

¼ cup white flour
⅛ teaspoon black pepper
2 pounds chuck steak

- Combine flour and black pepper. Rub flour onto meat until thoroughly covered.
- Sear chuck steak in bacon grease over medium heat until lightly browned on both sides. Remove from heat.

3 large carrots *(with peel),* **quartered**
1 large onion, quartered
6 sun-dried tomatoes
8 medium mushrooms, thickly sliced
1 rib celery, thickly sliced
¼ teaspoon dried thyme
1 bay leaf
1 quart water

- Preheat oven to 325°.
- Place meat in a large oven-proof soup pot *(or dutch oven)*. Add carrots, onion, tomatoes, mushrooms, celery, thyme and bay leaf. Add the water. Cover and cook in the oven until meat is tender, about 4 hours.

(continued on next page)

- Cool to room temperature.
- Carefully remove chuck steak from beef stock and reserve meat for later use. Using a large, finely meshed strainer, strain beef stock into a container *(with lid)*, discarding vegetables.
- Cover and refrigerate until cold. Skim the fat and discard.

	water *(as needed)*
2¾	**tablespoons cornstarch**
	salt *(to taste)*
	black pepper *(to taste)*

- Place beef stock in a four-cup measuring cup. Add enough water to the stock to equal 3 cups. Add the cornstarch and stir until dissolved.
- Pour beef stock into a medium saucepan. Cook and stir over medium-low heat until boiling. Boil 1 minute.
- Remove sauce from the heat.
- Season with salt and black pepper. Use immediately or refrigerate until ready for use.

makes 3 cups

Sourdough Starter

Sourdough starter is responsible for the wonderful texture and tangy flavor found in Sourdough Tortillas (recipe page 60). This starter can also be used to enhance the flavor of many yeast breads, muffins and biscuits.

2 cups white flour
2 cups milk
1 tablespoon sugar
1 teaspoon yeast

- In a one-quart container *(with lid)*, combine flour, milk, sugar and yeast. Stir well. Cover loosely. Store at room temperature for 3 days, stirring daily.
- After 3 days: Starter is ready for use, or can be refrigerated for up to 1 week. It is best *(but not necessary)* to let the sourdough starter warm up to room temperature before using, about 4 hours.
- After 1 week without use: Feed starter with ½ cup flour and ½ cup water. Stir, cover and return to refrigerator. *(This will keep the starter active for another 7 days.)*
- After use: Replenish starter by adding 1 cup flour and 1 cup water to the remaining starter. Stir well. Transfer starter to a clean container, cover and refrigerate.

makes approximately 4 cups

Notes

Index

Notes